Clay County Public Library

116 Guffey Street
Celina, TN 38551
(931) 243-3442

DRUG EDUCATION LIBRARY

PRESCRIPTION DRUGS

OPIOIDS THAT KILL

By Simon Pierce

LUCENT PRESS

Published in 2017 by
Lucent Press, an Imprint of Greenhaven Publishing, LLC
353 3rd Avenue
Suite 255
New York, NY 10010

Designer: Seth Hughes
Editor: Jennifer Lombardo

Cataloging-in-Publication Data

Names: Pierce, Simon.
Title: Prescription drugs: opioids that kill / Simon Pierce.
Description: New York : Lucent Press, 2017. | Series: Drug education library | Includes index.
Identifiers: ISBN 9781534560116 (library bound) | ISBN 9781534560123 (ebook)
Subjects: LCSH: Drug abuse–Juvenile literature. | Medication abuse–Juvenile literature.
Classification: LCC HV5809.5 P54 2018 | DDC 362.29–dc23

Printed in the United States of America

CPSIA compliance information: Batch #CW17KL: For further information contact Greenhaven Publishing LLC, New York, New York at 1-844-317-7404.

Please visit our website, www.greenhavenpublishing.com. For a free color catalog of all our high-quality books, call toll free 1-844-317-7404 or fax 1-844-317-7405.

Contents

The development of drugs and drug use in America is a cultural paradox. On the one hand, strong, potentially dangerous drugs provide people with relief from numerous physical and psychological ailments. Sedatives such as Valium counter the effects of anxiety; steroids treat severe burns, anemia, and some forms of cancer; and morphine provides quick pain relief. On the other hand, many drugs (sedatives, steroids, and morphine among them) are consistently misused or abused. Millions of Americans struggle each year with drug addictions that overpower their ability to think and act rationally. Researchers often link drug abuse to criminal activity, traffic accidents, domestic violence, and suicide.

These harmful effects seem obvious today. Newspaper articles, medical journals, and scientific studies have highlighted the many problems drug use and abuse can cause. Yet, there was a time when many of the drugs now known to be harmful were actually believed to be beneficial. Cocaine, for example, was once hailed as a great cure, used to treat everything from nausea and weakness to colds and asthma. Developed in Europe during the 1880s, cocaine spread quickly to the United States, where manufacturers made it the primary ingredient in such everyday substances as cough medicines, lozenges, and tonics. Likewise, heroin, an opium derivative, became a popular painkiller during the late 19th century. Doctors and patients flocked to American drugstores to buy heroin, which was described as the optimal cure for even the worst coughs and chest pains.

As more people began using these drugs, though, doctors, legislators, and the public at large began to realize that they were more damaging than beneficial. After years of using heroin as a painkiller, for example, patients began asking their doctors for larger and stronger doses. Cocaine users reported dangerous side effects, including hallucinations and wild mood shifts. As a result, the U.S. government initiated more stringent regulation of many powerful and addictive drugs, and in some cases outlawed them entirely.

A drug's legal status is not always indicative of how dangerous it is, however. Some drugs known to have harmful effects can be purchased legally in the United States and elsewhere. Nicotine, a key ingredient in cigarettes, is known to be highly addictive. In an effort to meet their body's demand for nicotine, smokers expose themselves to lung cancer, emphysema, and other life-threatening conditions. Despite these risks, nicotine is legal almost everywhere.

Other drugs that cannot be purchased or sold legally are the subject of much debate regarding their effects on physical and mental health. Marijuana, sometimes described as a gateway drug that leads users to other drugs, cannot legally be used, grown, or sold in half of the United States. However, some research suggests that marijuana is neither addictive nor a gateway drug and that it might actually have a host of health benefits, which has led to its legalization in many states for medical use only. A handful of states also permit it to be used recreationally, but the debate on this matter still rages.

The Drug Education Library examines the paradox of drug use in America by focusing on some of the most commonly used and abused drugs or categories of drugs available today. By objectively discussing the many types of drugs, their intended purposes, their effects (both planned and unplanned), and the controversies surrounding them, the books in this series provide readers with an understanding of the complex role drugs play in American society. Informative sidebars, annotated bibliographies, and lists of organizations to contact add to the text and provide young readers with many opportunities for further discussion and research.

AN OVERVIEW OF ADDICTION

The dangers of street drugs such as heroin and cocaine are well known, and although people still use them, many others avoid them because they are illegal. However, in the case of painkillers and other prescription medications, people may have a false sense of security because these drugs are legal and given to them or a friend by a doctor they trust. They assume these drugs are safe and may not even think of themselves as

being addicted because they can get the drugs from a pharmacy. However, their addiction is real and often has devastating effects on their lives and families.

Fortunately, according to the National Institute on Drug Abuse's 2015 Monitoring the Future survey, which tracks abuse of various drugs in young adults, prescription drug use is on the decline among young adults. However, this does not mean that it is not still a significant problem. Amphetamines are the most commonly abused prescription drugs, with 7.7 percent of 12th graders surveyed reporting that they had used them in the past year. Additionally, 5.4 percent had used opioids other than heroin, and 4.7 percent had used tranquilizers. These numbers

Pharmacists study for years to understand the interaction of drugs and the body. It is essential to use prescription drugs only as directed to avoid complications.

show that the only illegal drug more widely abused is marijuana, which 34.9 percent of 12th graders had used in the past year. Prescription drugs are taken inappropriately more often than drugs such as MDMA (ecstasy), LSD, or cocaine.

In some cases, people start abusing prescription drugs because they are given one by a friend or a drug dealer, or because they tried something in a relative's medicine cabinet, either to get high or to escape reality. However, in other cases, people become addicted after taking something that was legally prescribed for a legitimate medical issue. A person may have an accident and need to see a doctor for a prescription painkiller. Doctors will generally warn their patients that the drugs carry the risk of addiction, and that to avoid this, they should take the pills on a strict schedule—for example, one every six or eight hours. These patients often intend to stick to the schedule, but sometimes the effects of the drug will begin to wear off before it is time for the next dose. If the pain is very bad, someone may start taking a pill every four hours instead of six to avoid the time period between doses when they are in pain. When their painkillers are finished, they may find that because they have taken the pills too often, they are addicted. When a person who is addicted to painkillers stops taking them, he or she may experience symptoms of withdrawal because the body has become used to having the drug in its system. These symptoms include vomiting, muscle pain, diarrhea, and insomnia. The body's reliance on these medications is called physical dependency.

Sedatives, or tranquilizers, are also commonly abused prescription drugs. This type of drug is used to treat anxiety and insomnia (inability to fall asleep). Like painkillers, they are often abused after they are prescribed for a legitimate reason. Barbiturates, a type of sedative, are particularly dangerous because it is easy for someone to die from an overdose, which means taking too much of a drug. When combined with alcohol, this risk is even greater.

Benzodiazepines are another type of sedative. They are less dangerous than barbiturates because the risk of dying from an overdose is lower, but benzodiazepines can create a physical

Insomnia is a common symptom of mental illnesses. Lack of sleep can lead to a great deal of physical, mental, and emotional discomfort, which increases the temptation to abuse sedatives.

dependency that can lead to unpleasant withdrawal symptoms and a craving for more of the drug. Valium and Xanax are two well-known examples of benzodiazepines.

In the case of stimulants, which are often prescribed for narcolepsy (a sleep disorder that makes it difficult to stay awake) and attention deficit hyperactivity disorder (ADHD), the people most often abusing them are not those with a medical condition. Adderall and Ritalin are often prescribed legally to people with ADHD; if those people do not want to take all of their medication, they will sometimes sell it to others. Other people tell their doctor they have difficulty concentrating even when they do not so they can get a prescription, either to sell or to take themselves. These two medications are often abused by students—particularly college students—who want to be able to focus better and stay awake longer when studying for tests. Other people may use Adderall—a type of amphetamine—to lose weight or to improve sports performance, even though amphetamine use is banned in major sports leagues and the Olympics.

Addiction to prescription drugs can be overcome, but it is a long and difficult road for both the person who is addicted and his or her family and friends. It is not something that can be overcome simply by a desire to quit, although that desire is the first step. Addictive drugs can change the abuser's body and even alter the structure of the brain. Only with proper medical help can recovery truly begin.

Chapter One

THE HISTORY OF MODERN MEDICINE

Physicians have been an important part of all cultures for thousands of years. Early healers learned how different plants could affect the body and would give them to people who came to them asking for help in treating any diseases they had. Before medical schools were established, doctors experimented with cures on their own and passed that knowledge on to others who wanted to learn how to practice medicine. They did not know anything about bacteria or viruses. Many doctors in civilizations such as ancient Greece and Rome, as well as colonial America, believed the things that caused disease were too much or too little of the body's natural fluids. For example, if someone had a fever, a doctor might determine that this was because there was too much hot blood in the body and attempt to fix it by putting leeches on the patient to suck out some of the blood.

Due to the fact that there were no regulations for drugs or tests for doctors, it was easy for anyone to claim he or she was a doctor and cheat patients out of their money by giving them medicines that did not work or that ended up being harmful to them, although many doctors were genuinely interested in helping people. After medical schools became common, doctors started to become more highly regarded in societies around the world.

The Evolution of Modern Medicine

Medicines have often been discovered by trial and error. People would try a certain plant and keep using it if it worked or stop using it if it did not. However, early cultures generally did not restrict the use of these plants. Anyone could go find and take them if they knew where the plants grew and how to use them, although they often needed a healer to tell them this information. As time went on, doctors began to experiment with combining different plants and found that in some cases, certain plants worked better together than on their own.

Technology also advanced over time, allowing researchers to create laboratories where they could study plants and combine them to make new types of medications. For instance, a

Treatment of mental and physical ailments has been fundamental to all cultures. The general public has always relied on the knowledge and experience of trained healers.

common painkiller sold today is called Lortab. It combines hydrocodone, a strong painkiller that comes from the opium poppy, and acetaminophen, a weaker painkiller that was originally found in the bark of the willow tree. The acetaminophen makes the hydrocodone work better, so they were combined into one pill. Researchers were able to take the active ingredients out of plants and put them into liquid or pill form, rather than having patients chew on leaves or bark. The early 1800s were "a turning point in the knowledge and use of medicinal plants. The discovery, substantiation, and isolation of alkaloids from poppy (1806), ipecacuanha (1817), strychnos (1817), quinine (1820), pomegranate (1878), and other plants, then the isolation of glycosides, marked the beginning of scientific pharmacy."[1]

Many modern prescription drugs have been developed by studying natural remedies that were used for centuries. By distilling the chemicals found in traditional remedies, scientists have been able to develop powerful drugs to treat a variety of medical conditions.

As technology advanced even further, researchers no longer had to get compounds directly from plants. They began to make synthetic versions—drugs made completely in a lab. Many drugs today use synthetic versions of medicines that were originally taken from plants. Others are made from compounds that cannot be found in plants at all. These are the result of scientists experimenting with different compounds to see if any of them have a medical benefit. Many illegal, nonmedical drugs were discovered this way by accident. For instance, MDMA was created by the drug company Merck as it was trying to find a drug with a medical use. Instead, MDMA was created, which produces a high—feelings of well-being and happiness—but does not treat any kind of illness. MDMA cannot be found in nature; it must be created in a lab, although the different compounds that make it up can be found in various plants.

Is Natural Better?

Although technology has advanced to the point where scientists can make synthetic medications, many people do not trust these drugs and prefer to use natural remedies. Some minor illnesses can be treated this way. For instance, chamomile tea is widely used to help people fall asleep, soothe an upset stomach, and fight anxiety and depression. St. John's wort also has been shown to help with the effects of depression and has been used as far back as ancient Greece. Some people prefer to use herbal supplements, rather than synthetic medication, because there are fewer side effects with herbal remedies.

There is support for both sides of the natural versus synthetic argument. On one hand, it is true that natural remedies tend to have fewer side effects, but this is because they are often less powerful than synthetic medications. Synthetic drugs contain

Many conditions can be treated with both natural remedies and prescription drugs. It is important to listen to the advice of trained professionals when determining the best treatment plan.

compounds that are the same as the active ingredients found in plants, but at much higher concentrations, so they work more quickly. The drawback of such high doses is often stronger side effects and a higher risk of addiction. For instance, the effects of St. John's wort are similar to the prescription antidepressant Prozac, but St. John's wort is only recommended for people with mild-to-moderate depression. For severe depression, a prescription drug is typically recommended. St. John's wort also has similar side effects to Prozac, including dry mouth, headache, and dizziness, but they are often less severe. Some researchers believe this may also be a result of other compounds that are present in the plant, which are not found in the synthetic drug. These other compounds may work with the active ingredient to lessen the side effects. More research is needed to tell for certain.

The other side of the argument is that some conditions can be treated much more effectively with prescription drugs than with any of the herbs that doctors currently know about. For example, cancer is a deadly disease with no known cure. One treatment for cancer is chemotherapy, which involves strong doses of synthetic drugs. Some people claim that cancer can be treated or even cured with alternative medicine; for instance, Steve Jobs, the founder of Apple, believed he could cure his cancer by eating only fruit. Unfortunately, by the time he realized this was not working and agreed to try treating the cancer with drugs, it had spread to other parts of his body. It eventually killed him. Conditions that need to be treated quickly, such as anaphylactic shock (closing of the airways, generally due to an allergic reaction), severe depression that results in suicidal urges, or kidney failure need to be treated with strong prescription medications, although sometimes adding natural remedies can help with certain symptoms. Additionally, some people may find that prescription medication helps them control their illnesses better than natural remedies, even if their illnesses are not severe or life-threatening. The decision to take natural or synthetic remedies is a personal choice, and everyone is entitled to make the choice they feel is right for them.

Why Do Some Drugs Need Prescriptions?

In the United States, prescriptions were not required for any medication until 1914. Before that year, the drugs that were being produced were widely available; people did not have to visit their doctor to get them. Pharmacies sold drugs such as morphine and cocaine to anyone who wanted them, and they could even be ordered by catalog. Safety testing was also not required, so some very dangerous drugs were often sold by people who claimed that they could cure various illnesses.

Some of these people, like some of the untrained doctors in ancient civilizations, were trying to cheat people out of their money. They developed patent medicines—so called because in 17th-century England, where the first patent medicines were created, a royal endorsement was called a patent. These "medicines" often did not work at all and sometimes were actually harmful. For example, a product called Mrs. Winslow's Soothing Syrup, which was created to help soothe babies' teething pains, killed many children in the early 1900s because it contained opium. In 1906, the Food

Historically, there has been no shortage of individuals making false claims about the effectiveness of medical remedies. In the past, there was no way for a consumer to verify the contents or effectiveness of these "miracle cures."

and Drug Administration (FDA) was created to make sure the food and drugs people were selling would not hurt anyone. This is why prescription drugs today need to be tested and approved by the FDA. Herbal supplements are not considered drugs, so they are not tested. Some people believe this is because they are less dangerous, but this is not necessarily true. In the 1990s, for instance, a diet drug called ephedra—made from the herb of the same name—was taken by many people before it was discovered that the pill caused heart problems and other severe physical issues. The FDA can ban a supplement, but only after many people report health problems associated with it. Other supplements may be safe, but also may not have any real effects. Like patent medicine peddlers, some supplement companies are only concerned with the quickest, easiest way to make money.

OVER-THE-COUNTER DRUG ABUSE

Prescriptions are required for the most dangerous and addictive drugs, but just because a drug is available without a prescription does not mean it cannot be abused. One of the most commonly abused over-the-counter (OTC) medications is cough syrup that contains the ingredient dextromethorphan. In high doses, this drug can cause hallucinations and out-of-body experiences. This is because it acts on the same receptors in the brain as the illegal drugs ketamine—a tranquilizer used legally by veterinarians and often illegally used at raves or music festivals—and phencyclidine (PCP). The abuse of cough syrup is known as robotripping, a word that comes from the brand name Robitussin.

Cough syrup may not seem like a dangerous substance, but according to the National Institute on Drug Abuse (NIDA), "Dextromethorphan can cause impaired motor function, numbness, nausea or vomiting, and increased heart rate and blood pressure."[1] It can also cause poor decision-making, addiction, and, in rare cases, brain damage.

1. "DrugFacts: Prescription and Over-the-Counter Medications," National Institute on Drug Abuse, November 2015. www.drugabuse.gov/publications/drugfacts/prescription-over-counter-medications.

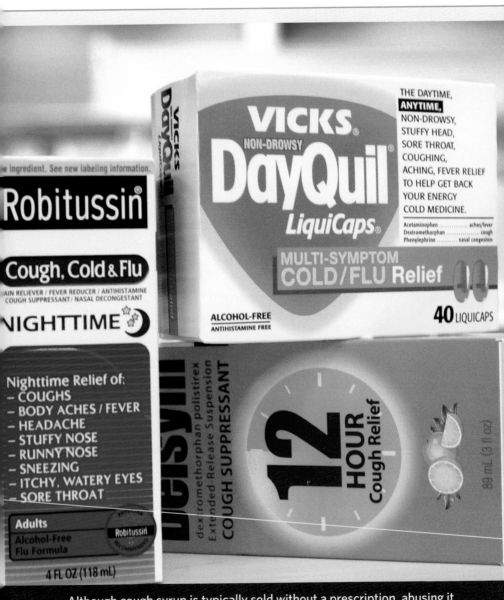

Although cough syrup is typically sold without a prescription, abusing it can be just as dangerous as abusing any other drug.

Opium and Opioids

Opium is a strong painkiller made from the opium poppy. Drugs that are made with this substance are called opioids. Some opioids are natural; they come directly from the poppy plant. These include morphine, codeine (two active ingredients in opium), and heroin. Laudanum—opium dissolved in alcohol—became very popular as both a painkiller and a recreational drug in the 19th century. Other opioids are synthetic, or made in a laboratory. Most addictive painkillers prescribed today are opioids, which are also known as narcotics. The term "opiate" was once used to describe the natural versions, while the term "opioid" was used to describe the synthetic versions. Today, the terms "opiate," "opioid," and "narcotic" are often used interchangeably. Sometimes there is confusion over what a narcotic is because the Drug Enforcement Administration (DEA) refers to all illegal drugs as narcotics. However, medically, a narcotic is a drug that depresses the central nervous system and makes people sleepy. Not all narcotics are opioids, but all opioids are narcotics.

In response to the dangers of the wide availability of narcotics, the federal government passed the Harrison Narcotics Tax Act in 1914. This law required a doctor's prescription for all narcotics. It also required doctors and pharmacists to pay a tax, as well as keep detailed records of patients who were given those medicines. In the 1970s, this law was replaced with the Controlled Substances Act, which separated drugs into different categories, or schedules, based on their properties. Opium and the strongest opioids were classified as Schedule II drugs, which are defined as "drugs with a high potential for abuse, with use potentially leading to severe psychological or physical dependence. These drugs are also considered dangerous."[2] Prescriptions are required for all Schedule II drugs.

Any drug can be dangerous if used incorrectly, and because prescription drugs are so powerful, they can be very dangerous indeed. The most frequently abused prescription drugs fall into three basic categories: painkillers, tranquilizers, and stimulants.

Chapter Two

THE RISE OF PRESCRIPTION DRUG ABUSE

In recent years, prescription drug use and abuse have risen dramatically. Drugs are being prescribed more often than in the past, leading to higher rates of abuse and addiction. According to a report by the Centers for Disease Control and Prevention (CDC) that looked at data from 2009 to 2012, 48.7 percent of Americans were taking at least one prescription drug, and 10.7 percent were taking at least five. There are many different opinions on why this may be. Some people believe it is because factors in the environment are making people sick more often than in the past. Others feel the problem is that doctors are too quick to prescribe drugs when a lifestyle change, such as more exercise or a change in diet, might work just as well. Some think this is the fault of the doctors or the pharmaceutical companies that market to them, while others believe it is the fault of patients who want a quick fix to their medical problems.

Until recently, prescription drug abuse did not receive the attention that abuse of illegal drugs does. Actor Robert Downey Jr.'s struggles with heroin and cocaine have made headlines, but the struggles of actors such as Carrie Fisher or Matthew Perry, who were both addicted to opioid painkillers in the past, barely registered. This neglect by the media and the public has led to a creeping epidemic that has spread across the United States.

The availability of prescription drugs greatly contributes to this problem. Many doctors are not well-informed about how to recognize the warning signs of addiction in their patients, or they do not have enough of a patient's medical history to realize that he or she is at greater-than-normal risk of becoming addicted. They may also not realize that some of the drugs they are prescribing are dangerously addictive; this was the case with Valium in the 1960s and, more recently, OxyContin.

With industrialized manufacturing techniques, prescription drugs can be easily and cheaply produced, then sold for a high profit.

Painkillers, tranquilizers, and stimulants can all have very important, legitimate medical uses. However, their use can become a problem when someone becomes addicted to them and begins using them to get through everyday life. This is a risk even when people take them correctly.

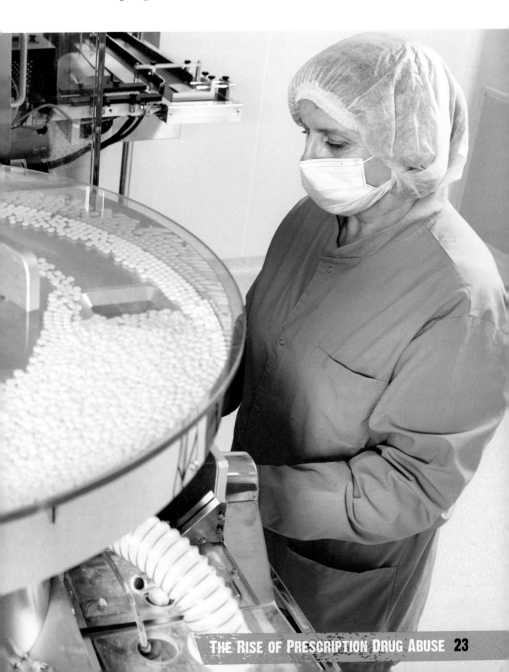

Opioid Painkillers

Opioids are very powerful and often quite addictive. The most infamous illegal opioid is heroin, a drug that is injected, smoked, or snorted by users. A weaker version of heroin is morphine, which has been used as a painkiller since the 18th century. Besides morphine, some commonly prescribed opioids include codeine, hydrocodone, fentanyl, meperidine, and oxycodone. The strength of these medications varies, so they are prescribed for different things. For instance, codeine is used to treat mild-to-moderate pain and can be found in some cough syrups. Many people believe it is more effective at treating coughs, although some studies have found this is untrue. Hydrocodone and oxycodone, which can be found in prescriptions such as Vicodin and OxyContin, are prescribed for more severe pain, especially back or joint injuries. Morphine is typically used only in hospitals because it is so strong, and fentanyl is up to 100 times stronger. It is even stronger than heroin, so it is generally reserved for only the most severe pain or for people who have developed a tolerance to weaker painkillers. While all these drugs can be safe if taken under a doctor's supervision, the potential for abuse is very real, especially if the patient has had a prior problem with addiction, either to another drug or to alcohol.

Opium abuse has long been recognized as a serious danger to society. In the 19th century, opium was a profitable trade good between China and Britain, but opium addiction devastated people from all walks of life.

Many people believe, due to the name "painkiller," that these drugs fix whatever is causing the body pain. However, this is a myth. What painkillers actually do is reduce the body's ability to feel pain. According to NIDA, "Opioids act by attaching to specific proteins called opioid receptors, which are found in the brain, spinal cord, gastrointestinal tract, and other organs in the body. When these drugs attach to their receptors, they reduce the perception of pain."[3] In some people, painkillers also create feelings of relaxation and extreme happiness, which can contribute to the risk of addiction. However, there are unpleasant side effects as well. These include "constipation, dry mouth, confusion, lack of coordination, lowered blood pressure, weakness, dizziness, [and] sleepiness."[4]

In addition to the physical side effects of painkillers, the body quickly becomes accustomed to the drug, and the user needs to

Symptoms of withdrawal have the potential to be worse than the original ailment. While prescription drugs can ease suffering, the consequences of abuse can be extreme.

take more and more of it to feel the good effects. This condition is called tolerance. Developing a tolerance can make stopping use of the drug dangerous if a person is not careful. When a person enters treatment and stops using opioids for awhile, their tolerance decreases, although they do not notice this happening because they are not still taking the drug. If the person relapses (gives in to their craving and takes the drug again), they often take the same amount of pills they used to take when they were using the drug regularly. However, since their tolerance has decreased, their body can no longer handle that amount, leading to a fatal overdose.

Users of many drugs, including opioids, also develop a dependence—the body begins to crave the drug, and the user needs to take it to not feel sick. Dependency is one of the reasons why opioid addiction is so hard to treat. When a person does not get the drug, he or she begins to feel very sick and go through withdrawal symptoms. Opioid withdrawal generally causes shaking, nausea, depression, and cold flashes.

Tranquilizers: Addictive Sleep Aids

Tranquilizers are drugs that depress, or slow, the functioning of the nervous system and brain. Because of this, they are often called central nervous system (CNS) depressants. CNS depressants are most often used to treat anxiety disorders and insomnia. People who become addicted are often using them to fall asleep—the body may grow dependent on the drug, which means people will stop being able to fall asleep without it—to ignore emotional pain, or to get high. Like opioids, CNS depressants may be abused because they can create feelings of strong happiness.

There are two main categories of CNS depressants: barbiturates and benzodiazepines. Barbiturates are the older type of this class of drug. They are very effective at sedating (making sleepy) the person who uses them, but they can be very dangerous. Barbiturate overdoses are often deadly, and the user must be very careful about consuming alcohol while using the drugs, as that can increase the risk of death.

Benzodiazepines—sometimes nicknamed "benzos"—are a newer class of drug. They create feelings of calmness and relaxation by attaching to receptors in the brain that work with a neurotransmitter (a chemical that sends signals from the brain to the nerves) called gamma-aminobutyric acid (GABA). GABA naturally helps people feel relaxed. When benzodiazepines attach to GABA receptors, the effects of the neurotransmitter are increased. The first commonly prescribed benzodiazepine was Valium (diazepam), which was approved for sale by the FDA in 1963. Marketed mainly toward women with anxiety, it quickly became the most widely prescribed drug in the United States. At first, it was thought that benzodiazepines were very safe—overdoses from them are almost never fatal unless they are mixed with alcohol or other drugs—but within 10 years, doctors realized it was possible to become addicted to them. Modern benzodiazepines include Xanax (alprazolam) and Halcion (triazolam). They are generally prescribed for short-term periods or for occasional, not daily, use. Side effects include "decreased attention span, impaired judgment, lack of coordination, lowered blood pressure, memory problems, [and] slurred speech."[5]

Some studies have found evidence that benzodiazepines may also cause long-term damage in the brain, making it difficult or impossible for a person to function without the drug:

One meta-analysis examining patients who had gotten off benzos found deterioration in every area of intellectual and cognitive testing it studied and suggested that the damage may be irreparable. And benzos may actually make your condition worse than before you started taking the drugs because they compromise your ability to deal with it, [psychiatrist Peter Breggin] said.[6]

More research is necessary to determine the accuracy of these results.

Withdrawal from CNS depressants can be difficult. Although benzodiazepines are generally considered safer than barbiturates, getting off the drugs must be done under the supervision of medical personnel. To abruptly stop taking them—going "cold turkey"—can cause seizures and other medical problems that can be life-threatening. It is important for people who are taking these drugs properly to gradually take less and less so that the body can slowly become accustomed to doing without the drugs again.

SIGNS OF ADDICTION

Addiction can happen so gradually that people are sometimes not even aware it is happening to them. They may deny it for a long time and pretend that everything is fine. Some signs that people should watch for in themselves and loved ones include:

- Thinking often about when they can next take their medication

- Taking medication more often than they are supposed to, or more pills at once than they are supposed to

- Finding a new doctor when the old one stops prescribing the medication

- Ordering pills online, stealing from others, or buying pills from a dealer or friend

- Getting angry when someone brings up the possibility of addiction

- Changes in sleep, mood, personal hygiene, or eating habits

- Missing work, school, and other responsibilities

- Getting into more fights with friends and family

- Losing interest in activities they once enjoyed

MYTHS ABOUT PRESCRIPTION DRUGS

Myth: Prescription drugs are always safe.
Fact: Like all drugs, prescription drugs can be dangerous if taken without a doctor's supervision. Many drugs, even those sold over the counter at drugstores, can be deadly if someone takes too much or takes them with other drugs. When a doctor wants to prescribe a new treatment, the patient should always ask about the risks and benefits of the drug before agreeing to take it.

Myth: Prescription drugs are not addictive.
Fact: Many prescription drugs can be quite addictive. People should never take more of any drug than their doctor recommends, and they should never take drugs that were not prescribed for them.

Myth: It is possible to stop taking prescription drugs at any time.
Fact: Many drugs that doctors prescribe build up in the body over time. Quitting suddenly can cause the body to go into shock as it is deprived of the drug. Patients should always follow their doctors' instructions for ending a prescription. In many cases, they will have to take smaller and smaller doses until their body is used to not having the drug anymore.

Some prescription sleep medications can cause tolerance, dependency, and withdrawal. One example is zolpidem, which is sold under the name Ambien. Ambien is not a benzodiazepine, but it works on the same receptors in the brain, so it has similar effects. It is less dangerous and less addictive than benzodiazepines or barbiturates, but this does not mean addiction is impossible. When people take insomnia medications for long periods of time, they often need more and more of the drugs to get the same effect. This may cause them to take too many pills at once—a behavior that can be deadly. Additionally, the person may not be able to sleep anymore without the drug.

Abuse of Stimulants

The opposite of CNS depressants, stimulants increase the functioning of the nervous system, as well as raise heart and respiration rates. Methamphetamine, also called crystal meth, is one type of illegal stimulant. Some stimulants are legally prescribed to treat conditions such as asthma (they help force open the constricted breathing passages of a person undergoing an asthma attack) and help obese people lose weight (they raise a person's metabolism—the rate energy is burned—and suppress appetite). However, stimulants can be very addictive. They can produce a powerful high and feelings of invincibility (the ability to do anything) and interfere with the user's ability to make decisions. However, once the high wears off, a user often feels very depressed and begins to abuse the drug to feel better again. Because of this, stimulants are only prescribed for a few specific conditions.

One condition where stimulants have been found to be effective treatment is ADHD. People with this disorder often have problems concentrating, paying attention to ordinary tasks, and focusing in general. Doctors use the stimulants Ritalin (methylphenidate) and Adderall (dextroamphetamine) to treat this disorder. Those who support their use claim that in small doses, these drugs improve a patient's ability to concentrate and actually calm him or her down—despite the fact that stimulants generally cause people to become more active. This is because

Total Number of Prescriptions for Stimulants* Dispensed by U.S.A. Retail Phamacies from 1991-2010

*excluding products containing modafinil and atomoxetine

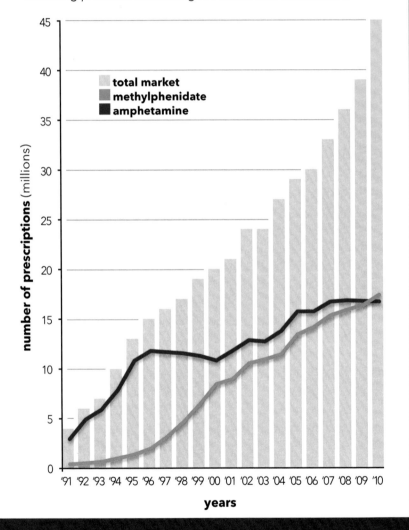

The number of stimulant prescriptions increased dramatically over a decade and a half, as this information from NIDA shows.

the drugs raise the levels of dopamine and norepinephrine, two neurotransmitters in the brain. Higher levels of dopamine cause feelings of happiness, and higher levels of norepinephrine increase the brain's ability to concentrate and make decisions.

Use of ADHD medications has become more controversial as doctors have increasingly prescribed them. Critics claim that Ritalin and Adderall are being given to patients who do not actually have ADHD, simply because parents and teachers want children to be quieter and easier to handle. Even among doctors, there is debate about whether too many children are being diagnosed with ADHD, since more people have been diagnosed with it in recent years than in the past. Some doctors explain this by saying that the condition is becoming better-known and more easily recognizable, so patients are being diagnosed with something that might have gone untreated in the past.

Another topic of debate surrounding ADHD is whether Adderall and Ritalin are prescribed too quickly. In some cases, the condition is so severe that medication is the best answer. In others, simple behavioral changes might work just as well:

> *For instance, accommodations at school such as seating the child near the teacher for increased eye contact, giving a daily report card with checks for desired behaviors, and giving frequent breaks can improve ... performance in school. At home, organizational strategies, a predictable routine, and behavioral charts can also help.*[7]

Some people oppose the idea of giving drugs to children for any reason, even if they might benefit from them, especially since stimulants are frequently abused. However, stimulants are most often abused by people to whom the drug was not prescribed.

Stimulants can be very dangerous drugs to abuse. Doctors say they are relatively safe when taken at the recommended dose, but people who abuse them often take more than they should. Additionally, the people who are prescribed these medications have conditions that the drugs are treating. People who abuse Adderall and Ritalin often do not have any medical condition, which changes how the drugs interact with the brain. According to TeensHealth:

> *When a person takes it either unnecessarily or in a way it wasn't intended to be used, such as snorting or injection, Ritalin toxicity can be serious. And because there can be many variations of the same medication, the dose of medication and how long it stays in the body can vary. The person who doesn't have a prescription might not really know which one he or she has.*[8]

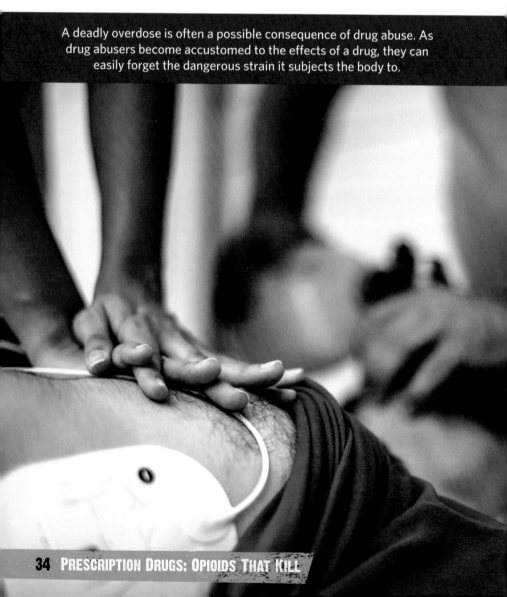

A deadly overdose is often a possible consequence of drug abuse. As drug abusers become accustomed to the effects of a drug, they can easily forget the dangerous strain it subjects the body to.

It is widely known that stimulants—especially Adderall—are misused by high school and college students who are trying to improve their grades. Because these drugs improve concentration, they help students focus longer on their homework and studying. Many people also believe that Adderall makes them smarter; in fact, research has proven that people who are given Adderall before a test think they are doing better on the test, but their scores remain the same. This myth that stimulants increase intelligence may lead people to take them unnecessarily.

Stimulants are also abused by people who take them to lose weight quickly. Without sticking to a healthy diet and moderate exercise, though, the weight quickly returns after the person stops taking the drugs. This may contribute to someone's continued abuse of these drugs.

Another way in which stimulants are abused is as a performance-enhancing drug. High school, college, and professional athletes sometimes use Adderall to increase their energy so they can run faster and longer. They also use it to increase their concentration. The use of performance-enhancing drugs in professional sports is not a secret; in baseball, especially, drugs such as amphetamines and steroids have been used for years. Seeing a professional athlete appear to get ahead in his or her field by using stimulants may encourage younger athletes to try them as well. However, abuse of Adderall to improve sports performance carries its own risks: Amphetamine increases heart rate, so someone who takes Adderall and then does a strenuous activity can increase his or her chance of heart attack or stroke.

Repeated abuse of stimulants can cause feelings of paranoia and extreme anger, as well as permanent damage to the heart and cardiovascular system. Stimulants can also cause a person to develop a dangerously high fever or even go into seizures. Overdosing may kill the user.

Painkiller Abuse: A Growing Epidemic

Although painkillers are not the only prescription drugs that can create addiction, their abuse has become a severe problem within the last 20 years. One of the first nationwide drug problems in the United States was an addiction to morphine among wounded veterans of the Civil War. Doctors of the time did not realize how addictive the drug could be and often overprescribed it when treating the soldiers. After doctors realized the problems opioids could cause, they tried not to prescribe them at all.

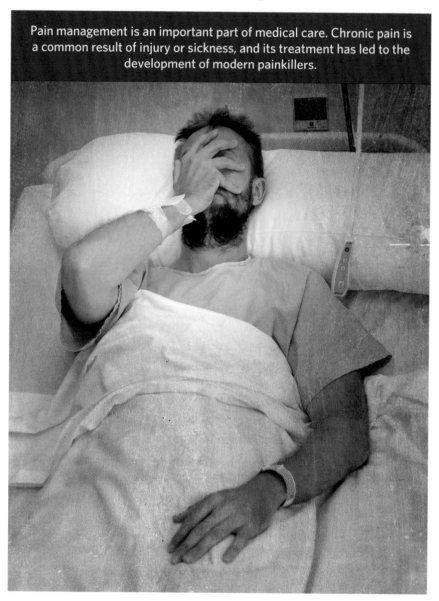

Pain management is an important part of medical care. Chronic pain is a common result of injury or sickness, and its treatment has led to the development of modern painkillers.

Unfortunately, this fear of prescribing opioids led to another problem: People with severe pain were not being given medication that could help them. According to Dr. David Thomas, a program officer with NIDA, "A lot of health care professionals did not want to prescribe opiates at all because they thought [if] you give the slightest amount, you turn your patients into addicts. And so even people with stage four cancer weren't being given opiates; they were left to suffer."[9] In attempting to correct this problem, the U.S. Secretary of the Department of Health and Human Services told doctors in 1992 that the addictiveness of painkillers was a myth and encouraged them to prescribe opioids more often for severe pain. Some drug companies took advantage of this statement by developing new painkillers and convincing doctors to prescribe them even for mild pain.

Problems with the Drug Industry

Drug companies often promote medications that they make by visiting doctors to tell them about the benefits of prescribing those drugs. They give doctors gifts such as pens, stuffed animals, and candy bars, all of which have the name of the drug they are selling on them. Some pharmaceutical representatives, also called drug reps, are knowledgeable, but others do not have a scientific background and do not know anything about the drug they are paid to promote. Most doctors are aware of this and will research the drug before prescribing it to patients, but some will simply take the representatives' word that the drug is safe, especially if they are swayed by the free gifts.

Some companies go even further than giving out pens and other small items. They may bring doctors lunch, take them out to dinner at expensive restaurants, or pay them to give speeches to other doctors about the benefits of a particular drug. This can create a conflict of interest for the doctor—he or she may prescribe a certain drug not because it is best for the patient, but because the doctor has been convinced to do so by a certain drug company.

With constant research and development, new drugs to treat a variety of ailments are always available. Pharmaceutical representatives educate doctors about newly available drugs, but they are also responsible for promoting the sale of these drugs.

In an effort to make people more aware of the conflicts of interest his or her doctor may have, a clause in the Affordable Care Act required the creation of a federal website called Open Payments Data, where people can see what type of benefits drug companies have given to doctors. This can help people be more informed when their doctor prescribes a drug for them.

Although the FDA approves drugs before they can legally be sold, some drug reps may try to convince doctors that their company's drug can be used for things other than what the FDA approved it for, a practice that is called prescribing off-label. Doctors are legally allowed to prescribe drugs off-label if they believe the drug will benefit their patient. However, some drug reps suggest prescribing drugs off-label without having any idea how they will affect someone who does not have the condition the drugs were approved for. They may suggest this only to boost sales of their company's drug.

The prescription painkiller epidemic was caused in part by Purdue, the makers of OxyContin. Purdue advertised OxyContin as the only painkiller that provided 12-hour pain relief, even though the company knew the drug wore off before 12 hours in many people. Purdue reps convinced some doctors to prescribe stronger doses of the drug so it would not wear off so soon. These stronger doses quickly got patients addicted. In 2007, Purdue was investigated by the federal government, admitted that it was guilty of lying about how addictive OxyContin is, and paid $635 million in fines.

Most doctors genuinely want to do the best thing for their patients, but they may be misled by the research that is published. Although all prescription drugs are required to be studied for safety and effectiveness before they can be sold, sometimes these studies can be manipulated to show a specific result. In 2013, *Science News* reported that the drug company Pfizer sometimes published false information:

Lisa Bero of the University of California, San Francisco, an expert in methods to assess bias in scientific publishing,

With any prescription, it is important for people to understand what they are taking and any possible side effects. Consulting a pharmacist or multiple doctors, as well as reviewing accurate sources of information, empower a patient to use prescription drugs safely and responsibly.

[said], "We know that entire studies don't get published and that what does get published is more likely to make a drug look favorable ... [Publishing false information] adds another layer."

In three of the 10 trials [that were reviewed for accuracy], the numbers of study participants in the published results didn't match those in the internal documents. In one case, data from 40 percent of the participants were not included in the published trial.[10]

Not every prescription drug is dangerous and not every study is wrong, but it is still important for people to be careful about the drugs they are taking, even if a doctor has prescribed them. Opioids can be useful for managing severe pain over a short period of time, but they should not be taken for minor pains, and the directions should be followed very carefully.

Unintended Consequences

It is not uncommon for someone to become addicted to more than one type of drug. This may include a mix of legal and illegal drugs; for instance, someone could be addicted to alcohol, which is legal, and marijuana, which is still illegal in some states and at the federal level. In the case of prescription drugs, multiple addictions can occur when a person is prescribed more than one addictive drug or becomes addicted to one drug and illegally obtains another to counter some of the first drug's effects. For instance, a person who is taking Adderall may have trouble sleeping, so he or she may take Xanax or another benzodiazepine at night to counter that effect. Even if someone does not become addicted to both drugs, mixing two different types of drugs can have consequences that the user did not think about beforehand.

Another serious risk that comes with abuse of prescription drugs is the potential for abuse of harder drugs. It has been proven that abuse of prescription opioids carries a high risk of heroin abuse; heroin is easier and cheaper to get and produces the same effects as painkillers, but much stronger.

Some experts are concerned that the abuse of stimulants may also lead to abuse of other drugs. Studies have shown that children with ADHD are more likely to abuse drugs such as nicotine and alcohol as they get older, but researchers are unsure of the exact reasons for this, so they cannot say for certain that it is because of the medications they take as children. Additionally, since Adderall and methamphetamine are very similar, people fear that someone who abuses Adderall may eventually turn to meth. Again, no clear link has been shown in this case.

Even if someone who abuses opioids or stimulants never turns to other drugs, the addiction to prescription drugs comes with many of its own problems for the user, as well as his or her friends and family.

Chapter Three

THE CONSEQUENCES OF ADDICTION

People often underestimate how addictive drugs are. Addiction to almost any drug starts slowly. If someone is using a drug to get high, they often believe they can try it once or twice and experience the drug's high without becoming addicted. However, the abuse of prescription drugs differs from the abuse of illegal drugs in that many users are first given the drugs legally by a doctor they trust. Some people take prescription drugs illegally to get high, but others use them only to treat a medical problem. Because of this, the descent into addiction can go untreated far longer than it would with other drugs.

Some people are shocked to find out that they have an addiction to a prescription drug. *Vogue* writer Kelley McMillan began taking the benzodiazepine Klonopin (clonazepam) after her psychiatrist prescribed it for her anxiety. She had grown up with a mother who used alcohol and prescription drugs to deal with the mental health issues she faced, so to McMillan, prescription drugs such as Klonopin seemed like a magic cure that would help her control her anxiety while avoiding becoming an alcoholic. She did not notice herself becoming addicted to Klonopin until her doctor mentioned it:

> [M]y doctor was concerned that during the previous six months, I'd refilled my Klonopin prescription early a few times, something she had to approve at each instance. Those early refills, she said, had caught her attention for possible abuse. I was stunned. Sure, I'd refilled my scrip early on occasion, but only by a couple of days, ten days, tops. This was due in part to my hectic travel schedule, but also to the fact that

I sometimes took a few more pills than prescribed, on nights when I couldn't sleep or days when I felt particularly anxious. I never took Klonopin to get high; I took it "as needed," as the label said to.[11]

McMillan, scared by her doctor's words, made an appointment with a psychiatrist who helped her reduce her Klonopin dose over the course of a year. She also made lifestyle changes to control her anxiety, such as cutting back on sugar and caffeine, exercising more, and getting more sleep. If she had ignored her doctor's warning, she may have ended up spiraling further into addiction.

Many people who are prescribed powerful drugs never abuse them or develop an addiction to them. By far, the majority of people take them for a while as prescribed and then stop using them. However, some people begin to abuse the drugs and, if not caught in time, become addicted to them. In the United States, prescription drug addiction is a serious problem. According to NIDA for Teens, "Prescription and over-the-counter drugs are the most commonly abused substances by Americans age 14 and older, after marijuana and alcohol."[12]

Risk Factors for Addiction

Anyone can become addicted to a drug. However, there are warning signs that a person may be more likely to develop a drug abuse problem. People who are already addicted to other drugs and alcohol or have been addicted in the past are very likely to become addicted, particularly to opioids or stimulants. Additionally, the risk of drug addiction is partially genetic, which means that people with family members who abuse drugs are more likely to abuse drugs themselves.

Childhood trauma and mental illness are two important risk factors for addiction. People who have been abused physically, emotionally, or sexually and have not seen a therapist to learn how to deal with emotions that often accompany abuse, such as shame, anger, or fear, may turn to drugs as a way to escape their problems. People with an untreated mental illness, such as

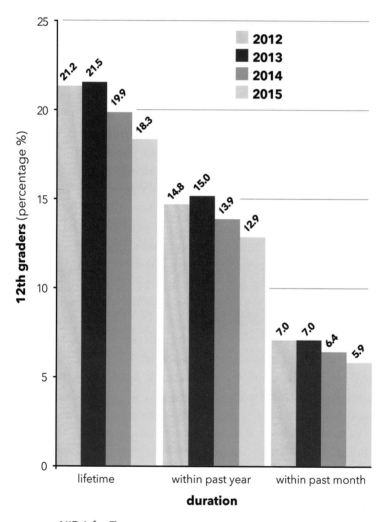

American 12th Graders Who Have Used Prescription Drugs Once or More from 2012-2015

Legend: 2012, 2013, 2014, 2015

12th graders (percentage %)

- lifetime: 21.2, 21.5, 19.9, 18.3
- within past year: 14.8, 15.0, 13.9, 12.9
- within past month: 7.0, 7.0, 6.4, 5.9

duration

source: NIDA for Teens

Although prescription drug abuse among 12th graders has been declining, it is still a serious issue.

bipolar disorder, depression, and anxiety, may also self-medicate this way. Unfortunately, the relief they experience is short-lived, and drug addiction causes more problems than it solves.

Unemployment can be a risk factor for addiction because people often feel bad about being unemployed. Many societies value a person's contribution to the workforce, so people who are unemployed may be seen as lazy, even though they often do not choose to be unemployed. Adding to their problems is the fact that if they are unemployed, they often live in poverty because they have no way of making money. The struggles of not having enough money and not being able to find a job may cause some people to turn to drug abuse out of a sense of hopelessness.

More women than men become addicted to prescription drugs, probably because they are two to three times more likely than men to be prescribed drugs such as sedatives. According to the British newspaper *Telegraph*, "One study found that 29 [percent] of women, compared to 17 [percent] of men, are likely to have been treated for a mental-health problem."[13] Researchers believe this is due to a combination of factors. One is that some doctors may believe women are more in need of medication to control their emotions. Another is that men may be less willing to seek help for mental or emotional issues because of pressure from society for men to appear strong and in control of themselves.

The prescription benzodiazepine Xanax has come under fire as one of the most commonly abused tranquilizers. Like Valium before it, it has been marketed as extremely safe and prescribed commonly for all sorts of complaints, notably anxiety, nervousness, and problems sleeping. However, like Valium, Xanax can be very addictive, and its over-prescription has made it readily available on the street, where people sometimes use it to come down from a stimulant high or deal with the effects of opiate withdrawal.

Age is another factor in determining the risk of addiction. Young adults are more likely to abuse drugs than people in other age groups because they are more likely to begin abusing drugs without fully understanding the consequences of abuse.

They are also likely to fall victim to "optimism bias"—the belief that bad things will not happen to them. People of all ages can have an optimism bias about the possibility of prescription drug addiction—or, in fact, any addiction. Often, young adults have this bias because they either do not personally know anyone who has become addicted to prescription drugs, or they do not know that someone they know is addicted because the person is hiding his or her addiction from friends and family. Young adults are also likely to be dealing with strong emotions. If they do not have a good support network of family and friends and have not learned how to deal with their emotions in a healthy way, they may turn to drug use.

Women are more widely prescribed medication for mental health problems than men. However, there is debate as to whether or not women actually have more mental health issues than men.

A Steady Supply of Drugs

A person who becomes addicted to any drug has many problems. The first is the need to secure a supply of the drug. People typically take larger than normal doses of the drug they are addicted to; in the case of prescription drug users, this means that a supply that is supposed to last them a month may run out much more quickly. People who are recovering from addiction often recall that the first thing on their minds when they woke up was how to get enough drugs to get through the day. Without enough drugs, they will suffer from withdrawal symptoms. Prescription drug abuse may first start when people take the drug to help with a problem, such as pain or emotional distress. Because their bodies build up such a tolerance to the drug, however, they need larger doses over time to make the drug work. In the case of painkillers, the users' bodies may have also developed a dependency on the drugs, which means that their bodies can no longer tolerate pain unless they are taking pills. Without the drugs, the original symptoms may return, or the users may experience withdrawal symptoms, making life doubly difficult for people who are addicted to prescription drugs.

People with a prescription drug addiction may not have to immediately turn to drug dealers, although many dealers do deal in prescription drugs. With a prescription, they can legally get the drugs they crave at a clean, safe pharmacy. The fact that what they are doing is legal leads many people to deny to themselves that they are addicted.

Getting a prescription can be difficult, however. Most addictive prescription drugs are carefully controlled and monitored. Doctors have to keep track of how often they prescribe these drugs to patients, not only for the health of the patient but also to make sure they do not become, in effect, drug dealers. Many people who take or sell prescription drugs illegally turn to a process known as "doctor shopping." In other words, they go to several different doctors all around the town or city they live in so that their prescription history goes unnoticed for as long as possible. They also look for doctors who will turn a blind eye to how often they are asking for refills. Emergency rooms are a good source of prescriptions, partly because the doctors there are often too busy to follow up with patients who come in. Sometimes a person who is addicted or a dealer who sells the drugs will go to hospitals or pain clinics complaining of severe pain so that a doctor will give them morphine or a prescription for a painkiller. In some places, doctors are so busy that they do not do tests on the patient and will simply take the patient at their word that the pain they are in is severe enough to need an opioid painkiller. Also, it is easier for patients to use fake names in an emergency room setting. As a last resort, some people steal or try to forge the prescription pads doctors use so that they can write as many prescriptions as they need.

Even when they get a prescription, dealers and people who are addicted must be careful about where they fill it. Pharmacies keep track of how often they can fill a prescription, for insurance purposes and to catch people who are trying to get large amounts of addictive drugs. People who are trying to illegally fill prescriptions must typically use many different pharmacies, being careful not to visit any one too often.

When young adults want to take prescription painkillers, barbiturates, or benzodiazepines to relax or get high, they may find them in their friends' or relatives' medicine cabinets. This is a cheap and easy way for them to get these medications, so while the price, difficulty, or risk of finding a dealer may prevent them from trying other illegal drugs, there are sometimes fewer barriers to prevent them from trying prescription drugs.

Prescriptions for stimulants are somewhat easier to get than prescriptions for opioids or sedatives. Not everyone who is prescribed Adderall or Ritalin shares his or her medication illegally, but some people see nothing wrong with it. Some of these people share willingly with friends to help them concentrate better or get a lot of work done quickly. Others take fewer pills themselves and sell the extras.

Sadly, health care workers are sometimes abusers themselves or willing sources for illegally acquired prescription drugs. Doctors and nurses face enormous pressure on the job, and they may begin to self-medicate, believing they will be able to control their

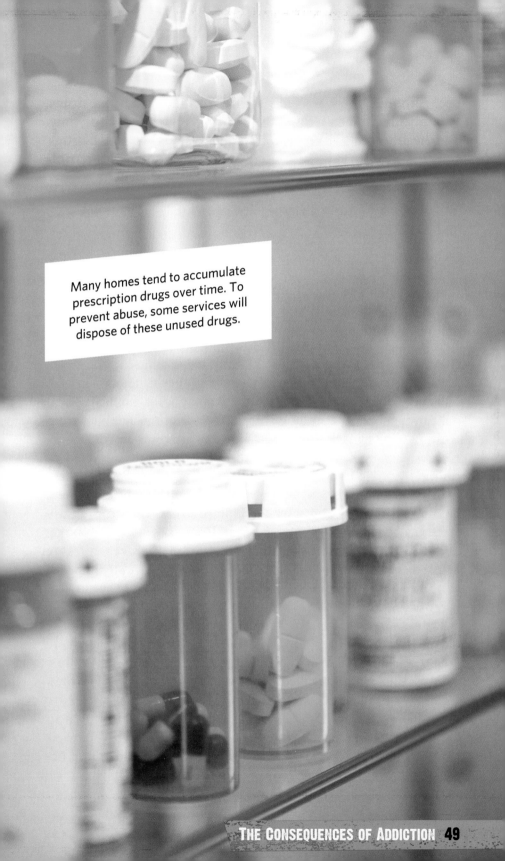

Many homes tend to accumulate prescription drugs over time. To prevent abuse, some services will dispose of these unused drugs.

use. Although there are tight controls on most addictive drugs, it is possible to get around them for a short period of time, and health care workers have frequent access to these drugs. Eventually, however, these users are caught, often with terrible consequences to their careers.

The Ease of Buying Drugs Online

The Internet has played a large role in making drugs more accessible. People can now order prescription drugs from the privacy of their own home, using a credit card to pay for the drugs. Some online pharmacies are legitimate, but many are not. These illegitimate pharmacy websites can be dangerous because they are operating outside the law, which means the government is not monitoring what they are selling. It is possible for these websites to lie about which drugs they are selling and send the buyer something completely different than what they ordered. This can have very dangerous effects on the person taking the drug.

Some people order their legal prescriptions online from legitimate pharmacies because the prices are often lower online. Others, however, want to find the drugs they are addicted to online in order to avoid having a pharmacy keep track of how many times they are buying those drugs. People who download an anonymous web browser are able to access the deep web— websites that are not found by search engines such as Google and Yahoo! Some websites that are part of the deep web are accessed every day by ordinary people. For instance, it is impossible to access someone's private e-mail account by searching for it on Google.

Other websites, however, are part of what is known as the dark web or dark net. The dark web consists of websites where illegal activities take place. It is possible for someone to buy drugs, guns, and other illegal items on these websites. The dark web can only be accessed when someone downloads a secure browser called Tor. Through that browser, data is encrypted so the user cannot be tracked by officials. People do not pay for their purchases with cash; the only accepted currency is called bitcoin, which is a digital form of money.

Unregulated markets on the Internet are convenient and anonymous avenues for people to purchase illegal drugs and to bypass government restrictions on prescription drugs.

The first major drug-selling website was called Silk Road. It operated from 2011 to 2013, when officials caught and arrested the man who had created it and shut it down. However, other sites quickly sprang up to replace it. Almost any type of drug can be found online, and the profits are huge. Kyle Soska, a researcher at Carnegie Mellon University, and his adviser, Professor Nicolas Christin, performed a study "that analyzed the size of dark net markets, finding they do brisk business, with relatively stable sales averaging $300,000–$500,000 a day." They also analyzed the types of drugs being sold and found that "marijuana consistently [accounted] for about a quarter of sales, followed by MDMA (more commonly known as ecstasy or Molly) and stimulants. Sales of psychedelic drugs, prescription medication and opioids are also significant, their research shows."[14]

Drugs are also available for sale through social networking sites such as Facebook. It is much easier to get caught this way than by using the more secure dark web, but that has not stopped many people. A Denver news station reported in 2016 that a secret Facebook group called Fly Society 420 had at least 900 members, most of them middle and high school students. Officials uncovered the group when the mother of one of the members checked her daughter's Facebook and reported the group to the police. The drugs the members talked about "included marijuana, marijuana concentrate, prescription drugs, LSD, and meth and ecstasy, among others."[15]

Addiction Takes Away Control

When addiction first begins, almost every person who deals with it is in denial. They tell themselves they are not addicted and can stop any time they want. For people who abuse prescription drugs, this denial period may go on longer because they will tell themselves that because a doctor prescribed it, they truly need the drug to treat their pain or the symptoms of withdrawal. Melissa Stetten, a writer for the website XO Jane, was prescribed Adderall by her doctor because her antidepressant made her tired. Adderall was supposed to give her more energy. It worked, but she soon became addicted to it. She described why she kept taking it:

My doctor told me to not take it on weekends, but I would wake up on Saturday feeling so tired and miserable, that the only way I could get out of bed was by taking Adderall. My life had gotten to the point where I had to basically take Adderall to concentrate on sleeping. So basically, I had to take Adderall to compensate for the way I felt after taking Adderall. It's like the circle of life for prescription drugs. I became a speed [methamphetamine] addict overnight.[16]

Stetten eventually stopped taking Adderall because she got to the point where she did not like the person she had become. Several years later, she tried it again when a friend offered her a pill, and she became addicted again. That friend later came to her apartment looking for Adderall because he had run out of his own supply. When she refused to give her pills to him, he pushed her up against a wall and stole her bottle of Adderall. After that incident, she again stopped taking the drug.

People who struggle with addiction can feel trapped and out of control. Some people who are addicted are fully aware of what they are doing to themselves but are unable to break the destructive habit.

DEFINING THE PROBLEM

People in the health care community use three different terms—misuse, abuse, and addiction—to describe the different ways people use prescription drugs improperly. They also make a distinction between dependency and addiction.

Misuse means using a drug incorrectly—for instance, treating a medical condition by taking something that was prescribed to another person.

Abuse means using a drug for reasons not related to its purpose, such as taking it to get high. Abuse may or may not lead to addiction, but it is dangerous.

Dependency means the body craves the drug after it leaves a person's system. Many prescription opioids and CNS depressants create a dependency in the body.

Addiction means a person has a mental dependency on the drug. They are always craving it and need it to feel "normal." People with an addiction will place getting the drug they are hooked on above all other concerns, even food.

Misuse and abuse of prescription drugs often lead to addiction. Addiction and dependency are sometimes used interchangeably because someone with an addiction typically also has a dependency on that drug.

An Expensive Habit

In addition to the physical and mental side effects that prescription drug abusers experience, they often face financial consequences. Although health insurance covers many types of prescription drugs, people who are addicted may pay for the drugs themselves to avoid creating a record of how often they are getting their prescriptions refilled. In addition, most insurance will only pay for a certain number of refills, so the person will eventually have no choice but to pay for the drugs on their own. If they get their drugs from a dealer, they obviously cannot use insurance for that expense. People who are addicted to prescription drugs often max out their credit cards and deplete their savings accounts to pay for the drugs. They may sell possessions, such as their car or jewelry, and they may lose their house or apartment if they are no longer able to make the monthly payments.

Prescription drugs can be very expensive. Prices vary depending on the type of drug, the number of pills, and the place where the prescription is filled. However, a bottle of pills can cost anywhere from $50 to $200 without insurance. If a person is taking several pills a day, a bottle that is supposed to last a month may end up lasting two weeks or less. Prescription drugs that are sold illegally cost much more. These prices also vary, depending on the drug. Oxycodone, for example, can range from $12 to $80 per pill. Adderall is typically sold for about $5 per pill, which can add up quickly when a person becomes addicted and feels the need to take it every day. Some people who are addicted to painkillers purposely injure themselves, breaking their bones or pulling out their own teeth so they can get a legal prescription.

Why Are Drug Prices So High?

Even with insurance, prescriptions for some drugs can be very expensive. They are much cheaper in other countries for a number of complex reasons. One major reason is that in the United States, drug companies set the prices for the drugs they make, while in other countries, the government sets the prices. Of course, many companies want to make as much money as they can, so it is common for them to charge more than the drug is worth. They typically claim the prices are so high to cover the cost of researching and creating the drug, but studies have found this is untrue. Often, the research is funded by government grants, so the companies are not actually paying much for it.

Another reason is that name-brand drugs cost more than generic versions. A generic pill is exactly the same as a name-brand pill, the way a Nike sneaker is the same thing as a shoe. For instance, Purdue created and sold OxyContin, the brand-name version of oxycodone. No other company could make a generic version of oxycodone until Purdue's patent—a government license that allowed Purdue to be the only company producing oxycodone—ran out. Some patents are good for more than 20 years. According to *TIME* magazine, drug companies will sometimes use unethical tactics to keep generic medications off the market. For example, they might release the exact same pill with a different coating so that they can reset the patent. In 2016, researchers at Harvard Medical School released a study that found that "drug prices decline to 55% of their original brand name cost once there are two generics on the market and to 33% of original cost with five generics."[17]

Another problem that drives up the price of prescriptions is that the FDA approval process takes a long time. The Harvard study found that "[a]pplication backlogs at the FDA have led to delays of three or four years before generic manufacturers can win approval to make drugs not protected by patents."[18] This means that even if a patent has expired, the brand name may remain the only drug on the market for several years while the FDA works through applications to make generic versions.

Consequences to Society

Prescription drug abuse affects the entire community in ways that extend far beyond the suffering of the addicted person or the pain it inflicts on his or her family. Some of the effects are the same as those caused by any drug's abuse, but some are particular to the abuse of prescription drugs.

One obvious effect is the increase in crime. When their insurance runs out, people who are addicted to prescriptions will often do just about anything to get the drugs they crave. When they run out of money, they often sell their belongings. When they have sold everything they can, they may begin stealing money or things to sell in order to buy more drugs. They may also commit insurance fraud—for example, forging

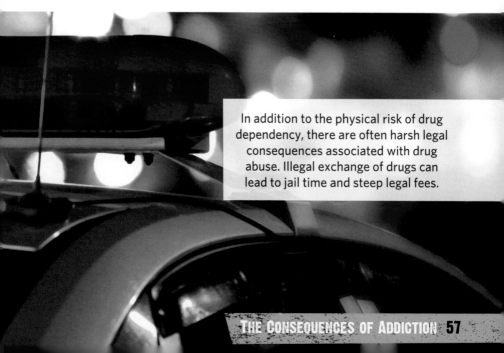

In addition to the physical risk of drug dependency, there are often harsh legal consequences associated with drug abuse. Illegal exchange of drugs can lead to jail time and steep legal fees.

prescription refills. These people may not realize they're committing a crime because they are not directly affecting an individual, but the truth is that when insurance companies lose money, they raise the rates of their services for everyone. People who are abusing or selling drugs may also become violent. People have been known to assault or even murder each other over drugs.

Prescription drug abuse impacts the health care system of a region. People who are suffering from withdrawal or who accidentally overdose need to visit the emergency room more frequently. People who abuse or sell prescription drugs also use up time that could be spent treating other patients. One reason why doctors sometimes do not take the time to check a patient's prescription history properly is that they are so busy seeing patients all day, they do not have a lot of time to spend with each individual. Doctor-shoppers add to the number of patients a doctor has to see, which means the doctor may have less time to spend with people who have come in for legitimate medical care.

Not every person who becomes addicted turns to crime or becomes violent, but the possibility exists. Even when they do commit a crime to support their habit, they often feel very guilty about it. Their body's craving for the drug is so strong that they often feel they have no other choice.

Seeking Treatment Is Crucial

For someone who is addicted to a drug, one of the hardest things to do is admit that he or she has a problem and seek professional help. He or she may fear being seen as weak or out of control, or at worst, a bad person. It is important to remember that no one chooses to become addicted to something. Changes in the way society views people struggling with addiction may encourage more people to come forward and seek help for their problems. Recovery can be a long and difficult road, but people who have gone through the process often say it is one of the best things they ever did.

Anybody can become a victim of addiction. It is important to pay attention to friends and loved ones for unusual changes in behavior. Escaping abuse can be a monumental task, and providing support for someone in need often makes the difference between success and failure.

PAINKILLERS:
A GATEWAY TO HEROIN

The high price of prescription drugs is one major reason why people who are addicted to painkillers end up turning to heroin. In many states, a bag of heroin costs between $5 and $10. A bag contains more than one dose of heroin, so buyers get more for their money than when they buy one pill of a drug such as oxycodone. Additionally, the effects of heroin are stronger and last longer than prescription painkillers. According to the *Washington Post*:

In the last few years, price has largely been determined by concerted action on the part of Mexican drug cartels, which previously controlled a smaller part of the U.S. heroin market, generally in the west ... Knowing that opiate pills such as OxyContin have become too expensive on the street, the cartels did two things: they dramatically increased production, and they developed networks to move it east of the Mississippi, [DEA special agent Joseph Moses] said.[1]

Drug cartels are able to provide a lot of heroin. The wide availability keeps the price from going up, even though many people want to buy it.

1. Lenny Bernstein, "Why a Bag of Heroin Costs Less than a Pack of Cigarettes," *Washington Post*, August 27, 2015. www.washingtonpost.com/news/to-your-health/wp/2015/08/27/why-a-bag-of-heroin-costs-less-than-a-pack-of-cigarettes-2/.

Chapter Four

RECOVERY FROM ADDICTION

The most important step in overcoming addiction is for the person to want to stop being dependent on the drug. Forcing someone into rehabilitation therapy—often called rehab—does not work because rehab requires people to actively work at overcoming their addiction. People who do not want to be there will not try hard enough to learn how to live without their drug of choice.

For many people, admitting they have a problem only happens when they realize they are no longer in control of their own life. This may be when they lose a close friend, lose their job, or simply realize that they are craving the drug too much. Many people will be ready to start the recovery process when they understand that the pain their addiction is bringing them and their loved ones needs to be dealt with.

Stigma Surrounding Addiction

Many people who are addicted to drugs are afraid to tell their friends and family because of the stigma—society's disapproval—surrounding addiction. People commonly believe that people who have an addiction are bad people, especially if they have done things such as stealing to support their drug habit. They also may have the idea that people who struggle with addiction are weak, and that if they were stronger, they would overcome their addiction or simply not have become addicted in the first place. Some people believe that a person who is addicted is not entitled to things that sober people are entitled to, such as vacations or privacy. For instance, they may feel that someone who is addicted should be watched at all times or their spending should be monitored. This erodes trust and makes a person with an addiction feel even more like a bad person. Other myths about people with addictions include:

- They are all criminals

- They do not want help

- They cannot hold down a job

- Everyone who tries to quit will relapse

- Someone who relapses has failed at recovery

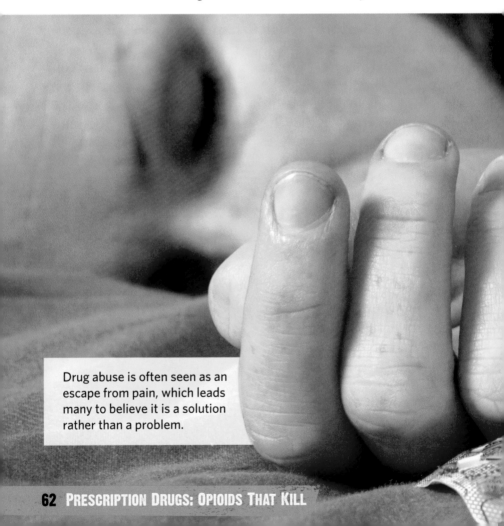

Drug abuse is often seen as an escape from pain, which leads many to believe it is a solution rather than a problem.

These myths about addiction can make it very difficult for people to admit they are addicted or have relapsed in their treatment. They may want to ask for help, but do not because they fear the judgment of friends, family, and society in general. This keeps them stuck in a cycle of addiction for much longer than necessary. In truth, anyone can become addicted to drugs, and being addicted does not make someone a bad person. It is not a choice anyone makes; it is simply their body's reaction to the drug. Admitting the problem and seeking treatment is much easier when the person does not feel personally attacked.

Opioid Withdrawal

The first thing that happens when a person enters recovery is ending the physical dependence on the drug, a process called detoxification, or detox. The drug must be completely removed from the user's system. This means going through withdrawal, which is why this part of the treatment is best done in a medical setting. Often, doctors will help the patient by giving him or her smaller and smaller doses of the drug in order to wean the body from its dependence. Even so, the physical symptoms of withdrawal will probably occur at some point, and these can be intense and debilitating.

Many drugs share similar withdrawal symptoms, but some are unique to specific drugs. For opioids, the withdrawal symptoms may be mild enough to be confused with the flu if someone has not been taking the drug for very long. People who have been dependent on it for longer will experience worse symptoms. In the first 24 hours after someone stops taking the drug, he or she may experience "muscle aches, restlessness, anxiety, lacrimation (eyes tearing up), runny nose, excessive sweating, inability to sleep, [and] yawning very often."[19] After the first day, a longtime user may experience worse symptoms, including "diarrhea, abdominal cramping, goose bumps on the skin, nausea and vomiting, dilated pupils and possibly blurry vision, rapid heartbeat, [and] high blood pressure."[20] Depending on the person, it takes about three days to a week for the drug to fully leave the body.

If opioid withdrawal is not severe, it can be treated at home with mild pain medications such as Tylenol, as well as rest and hydration. If it is severe, typically a person will need to be hospitalized and treated with stronger medications. One such medication is clonidine. It has been found effective at reducing opioid withdrawal symptoms by up to 75 percent. Another type of medication is suboxone, which combines a mild opioid and an opioid blocker to create a shorter withdrawal period.

Controversy Surrounding Methadone

Methadone is a commonly used drug that helps people gradually reduce the amount of opioids in their system without getting them high, similar to the way a person trying to quit cigarettes will use a nicotine patch. However, many people oppose methadone clinics because of the stigma surrounding methadone. The Partnership for Drug-Free Kids says that "many myths about its use persist, discouraging patients from using methadone, and leading family members to pressure patients using the treatment to stop."[21] These myths include the belief that methadone should not be used because people will simply get addicted to methadone instead of painkillers, that it has permanent negative side effects such as tooth decay, or that it makes the user unable to have children.

The federal government dictates that methadone must be given through licensed clinics. Some critics have stated that the regulations these clinics have are too strict and interfere with a patient's daily life. For instance, patients are required to come to the clinic daily to get their methadone, but the hours they are open "often conflict with patients' work schedules, and make it very difficult to take a vacation. In some areas of the country, the clinics are few and far between, requiring traveling many miles each day."[22] This is partially because people oppose methadone clinics so strongly that many people do not want one in their neighborhood. Society's negative views of people who have an addiction, even ones who are receiving treatment, also make many people unwilling to be seen entering or exiting a clinic. Reducing the stigma surrounding addiction and methadone use is an important way to encourage people to seek help for their addiction.

Benzodiazepine and Barbiturate Withdrawal

Some of the most difficult drugs to stop using are benzodiazepines and barbiturates. These have very long half-lives (the period of time it takes for the amount of drug in the body to be reduced in half), and the body itself becomes very dependent on these drugs. The process can be much more painful and dangerous than withdrawal from other drugs, and it may take months to fully complete the process. Besides symptoms such as anxiety, suicidal thoughts, hallucinations, muscle cramps, and vomiting, people going through withdrawal from these drugs may experience a life-threatening rebound effect. Because the drugs work by suppressing dopamine, adrenaline, and serotonin—neurotransmitters that make people anxious or excited—stopping use of the drugs all at once can flood the system with these neurotransmitters, which can overload the body. The symptoms of benzodiazepine withdrawal can be so severe that they sometimes kill the patient.

There are some medications that can be used to treat the specific symptoms of benzodiazepine and barbiturate withdrawal, but unfortunately there is no way to treat the overall withdrawal syndrome other than gradually reducing the amount of the drug a person is taking. This is one reason why the process takes so long. Sometimes another benzodiazepine or barbiturate can be used, but typically that just transfers the addiction to the new drug, so many experts discourage this method.

Stimulant Withdrawal

Because amphetamine is a stimulant like cocaine, many of the withdrawal symptoms are the same for both drugs. These include "fatigue; insomnia or hypersomnia [sleeping too much]; ... increased appetite; and vivid, unpleasant dreams"[23] within hours or days after stopping use of a drug such as Adderall. Withdrawal from Ritalin may include dizziness, decreased motivation, mood swings, nausea, and anxiety. Irritability and depression are also commonly reported symptoms of stimulant withdrawal. Many people try to stop taking the drug on their own, without seeking treatment, but in these cases relapse is very common. People who relapse typically begin taking the drug again because they are bored, it is widely available, or they are trying to treat their withdrawal symptoms.

According to the Australian Department of Health, "Animal and human studies have confirmed that the methamphetamine withdrawal syndrome may be protracted (the mood disturbance may last up to a year in some cases) and tends to be more severe than cocaine withdrawal."[24] This highlights the fact that

BABIES WHO ARE BORN ADDICTED

When a woman is pregnant, she transfers everything she puts into her body to her child. This includes good things, such as nutrients, as well as bad things, such as alcohol or drugs. Many people understand that a woman should not drink or do drugs, such as cocaine or heroin, while she is pregnant, but because prescription drugs are often viewed as safe, people may overlook that they can also have negative effects on an unborn child. A baby who is born addicted to prescription drugs may experience withdrawal symptoms after it is born, including "digestive issues, poor feeding, dehydration, vomiting [and] seizures."[1] The child may also not weigh enough at birth, which affects future mental and physical development.

1. Christine Case-Lo, "Opiate Withdrawal," Healthline, October 20, 2015. www.healthline.com/health/opiate-withdrawal.

prescription drugs can be just as dangerous as street drugs. As with benzodiazepine and barbiturate withdrawal, there is no one medication to treat stimulant withdrawal syndrome. Instead, medication may be given to treat various symptoms.

Overcoming Psychological Dependence

Treatment for physical dependence is only half of the recovery process. The other half is treating the psychological dependence on the drug. For a long time, addiction to the drug created stress in the person's life—stress that he or she dealt with by taking more drugs. He or she must now learn how to cope with stress without taking the drug. Counseling is vital to this process; someone who is recovering from addiction needs to be able to speak with other people who understand what he or she is going through in order not to relapse. Support groups such as Narcotics Anonymous provide great help for people in recovery.

One important tool for people recovering from addiction is cognitive behavioral therapy (CBT). This type of therapy was originally created to help people who suffer from alcoholism, and it was later altered to work for people facing different types of addiction, as well as mood disorders such as anxiety and depression. CBT teaches patients to change their thought patterns in order to change the way they experience stress and negative emotions. People who become addicted to prescription and other drugs are often using the drug to cope with feelings such as loneliness, depression, anxiety, or stress. CBT teaches them how to deal with those feelings on their own, without turning to an outside source. Techniques include "exploring the positive and negative consequences of continued drug use, self-monitoring to recognize cravings early and identify situations that might put one at risk for use, and developing strategies for coping with cravings and avoiding those high-risk situations."[25]

It is much easier to form a habit than it is to break it. It takes determination and dedication to recover, but it is never impossible.

Overcoming addiction is sometimes a lifelong struggle for the person who has a drug problem. Many people falter along the way and have to repeat the process several times. However, with a sincere desire to get clean and the support of medical personnel and other people who have gone through treatment, it is possible to make a full recovery and live a normal life again, although the person will always have to avoid that drug in the future.

Awareness Is Growing

For years, many people did not know that prescription drug abuse was a growing problem in the United States. Recently, it has become more commonly reported in the news, so people are starting to become more aware of the risks associated with the drugs they are prescribed. The DEA has always investigated claims of insurance fraud and prescription drug abuse, but recently it has taken further steps to crack down on this issue. Additionally, medical organizations have taken steps to educate doctors and the public about the risks of prescription drugs. Time will tell if these efforts are effective.

Chapter Five

THE FIGHT AGAINST PRESCRIPTION DRUG ABUSE

Prescription drug abuse is a problem for the abusers, their families, and society in general. It leads to more crime, higher death rates, loss of jobs, and poor school performance. Prescription drugs are increasingly common in the lives of young adults; even if they are not prescribed the drugs themselves, there is often some kind of pill in their parents' or friends' parents' medicine cabinets. This has led officials to be more aggressive in tracking down people who use and sell prescription drugs and educating people about the dangers of medicines they once considered safe.

Because prescription drugs can be so powerful, the federal government carefully regulates them to make sure that only doctors who have had the proper medical training needed to administer drugs can legally prescribe them. Even then, the government puts limits on the amount that can be given to a person over a given period of time.

Cracking Down on Drug Abuse

In recent years, many states have begun extensive programs to track the use of prescription drugs. These programs seek to cut down on the abuse of drugs by identifying people who have become addicted. They also hope to find doctors who are mis-prescribing the drugs and pharmacists who are illegally dispensing them.

A major tool in these monitoring programs is electronic data transfer (EDT) systems that immediately transmit information about a prescription to a central database. This allows

Electronic databases for prescription drug sales are an invaluable tool for law enforcement. By monitoring purchases, drug enforcement officials have a better idea of where to direct efforts to find individuals reselling prescription drugs illegally.

government officials to easily track data, such as the amount of drugs prescribed by a doctor or the number of prescriptions a patient has had filled.

These programs can be very successful in combating drug abuse. However, it is important to remember that these programs only work if they are actually used. In 2014, the Oklahoma Policy Institute reported that Oklahoma still has a painkiller epidemic, partially because many doctors do not use the Prescription Monitoring Program (PMP) before they prescribe drugs. In 2013, "Oklahoma prescribers only checked the PMP for one in every six prescriptions. Doctors claim that checking the PMP takes too much time, and undermines their authority as doctors to know what's best for their patients."[26]

From 1972 to 2016, New York State used a government-regulated prescription program. Under this program, special forms with serial numbers on them were used to prescribe drugs, and copies were kept by the state. Originally, the program was only used for Schedule II drugs, but it was expanded several times. In 1989, benzodiazepines were added to the program, and in 2004, all prescription drugs were included. The program helped track not only patients who were doctor-shopping, but also the doctors who were prescribing them medications. The program was aimed at reducing insurance fraud—people using insurance to pay for medications they did not need for medical reasons—but it also helped identify people who needed help with their prescription drug addiction. As of 2016, the program has been replaced by an EDT system; all doctors are now legally required to submit their prescriptions online.

Drug monitoring programs have their critics. Some have said that by creating extra paperwork and monitoring, these systems keep doctors from prescribing drugs to patients who could use them because they do not want the extra hassle or do not want to be examined by state regulators. This issue especially comes up with painkillers, which many people say have historically been under-prescribed out of fear of causing addiction.

Other people have criticized New York State's prescription program in particular because while benzodiazepine prescription did decrease after 1989, prescription of other, potentially more dangerous drugs increased. Some experts feared that doctors were prescribing untracked prescriptions in place of benzodiazepines, which may be one of the reasons why all prescriptions were added to the program in 2004.

It is important to note that the waves of OxyContin abuse that occurred in several states during the late 1990s and first years of the 21st century were most severe in states without any prescription monitoring programs, such as Virginia. However, it is also worth noting that Purdue sent representatives to those states to assure doctors that the drug was helpful, not harmful. They convinced many doctors that the problem was because people were taking the pill incorrectly, when really the problem was that the pill did not work as advertised.

Going After Drug Providers

Beyond merely tracking the writing of prescriptions, law enforcement professionals also investigate and try to uncover activities that allow people to abuse prescription drugs. In large cities, the police may have a special task force or department dedicated to cracking down on prescription drugs; most states have their own investigative departments as well. They concentrate their efforts in three areas: finding people who are trying to get drugs for themselves, finding dealers who are trying to get drugs to sell to others, and finding health care workers who are abusing prescription drugs.

Doctor-shoppers are generally detected either through drug monitoring programs or by doctors or pharmacists they have tried to get drugs from. They may have obvious signs of addiction or make enough visits to attract the suspicion of health care providers. These people are arrested for violating the laws governing the amount of drugs they are allowed to be prescribed.

Doctor-shoppers will take advantage of a lack of communication between doctors. By visiting multiple doctors, they are able to have multiple prescriptions filled without having an individual doctor suspect the possibility of abuse.

Dealers are the most frequent doctor-shoppers. They may also steal their supply from hospitals or drugstores, forge prescriptions, and counterfeit their own prescription pads. A 2012 study published in the *Drugs: Education, Prevention, and Policy* journal found that most high school students get their drugs illegally through dealers. Another study found that 56 percent of 11th graders in the state of Delaware reported buying drugs illegally from street dealers. Adults may not go through dealers as often, but they are still a significant source of prescription drugs.

It is a sad but true fact that doctors and nurses tend to have higher prescription drug addiction rates than the general public. The stress of their jobs, combined with the availability of drugs, can prove to be tragic for many. The *Journal of Addiction Medicine* interviewed 55 doctors in 2013 about their addiction to prescription drugs. Of those 55, "38 doctors (69 percent) abused prescription drugs. In describing their motivation, most said they turned to prescription drugs to relieve stress and physical or emotional pain."[27]

Far more dangerous, of course, are those doctors who write prescriptions for people they know do not need the drug to treat a medical problem; these doctors are the target of the doctor-shoppers. Additionally, some dealers may make bargains with doctors who are addicted to prescription drugs because doctors are not allowed to write prescriptions for themselves for controlled substances. One dealer who was a participant in the 2012 *Drugs: Education, Prevention, and Policy* study said, "I got a doctor who's a methadone junky. He can't write himself a script. But let's say you go in and you say, 'Listen, I need you to write me a script for 60 Percocets' … He'll go ahead on and write me one for 30 methadones, too. Then I get the Percs, he gets the methadone."[28]

Some doctors make it very easy for people to get a prescription, so although they might not knowingly be helping someone with an addiction, they are still making the drugs available to anyone who wants them. *Self* magazine told the story of a young woman named Michelle who became addicted to Adderall and found it very easy to get a prescription. "I went to see a doctor who asked me a few simple questions, like if I had a hard time concentrating or if I often lost things," she said. "I answered yes and left with an Adderall prescription. It was that easy." After her prescription ran out, she asked to be referred to a different doctor. According to Michelle, "He was basically a script doctor. He'd see you for 15 minutes, and you'd leave with whatever you wanted."[29] Although this doctor may not have known that Michelle was addicted to Adderall, he did not seem to care enough to find out, which helped her continue getting the drugs she wanted.

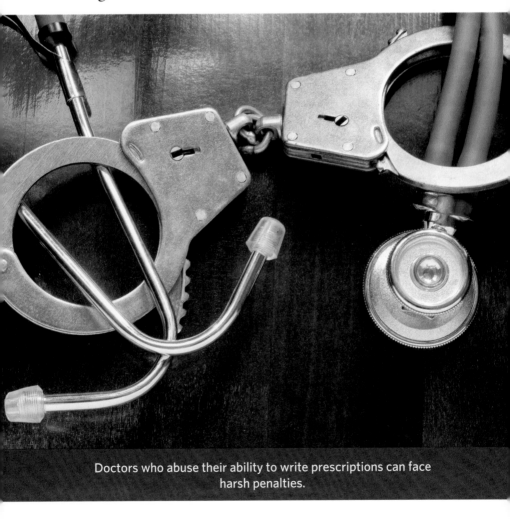

Doctors who abuse their ability to write prescriptions can face harsh penalties.

Doctors who mis-prescribe prescription drugs face stiff penalties. They may lose their DEA license, or even their medical license, and be unable to work as physicians. Also, they may face criminal charges and have to serve time in jail. Depending on what they have done, they may face both federal and state prosecution. Finally, if people died because of drugs obtained improperly, the prescribing physicians may even be charged with murder. Even if they avoid criminal charges, they may be sued. Pharmacists face similar penalties for filling illegal prescriptions, or for illegally selling drugs without a prescription. They are licensed and regulated by the DEA, and the amount of drugs they dispense is monitored and recorded.

Laws to Control Prescriptions

Schedule II drugs, such as opioids, can only be prescribed by doctors with a permit from the DEA. The drugs are also tracked by the federal government to make sure they are not stolen or sold on the street. Stimulants such as Adderall and Ritalin also belong to this class.

Benzodiazepines are Schedule IV drugs and not as strictly regulated. Schedule IV drugs are defined as "drugs with a low potential for abuse and low risk of dependence."[30] This does not mean no one can get addicted to them, just that they are less dangerous. Patients should take care when using these drugs, especially given the dangers of withdrawal from them. In truth, any drug on the federal schedules must be used with caution.

Each of the drug schedules comes with a limit on the amount of a substance a person can legally have. For Schedule II drugs, the limit is a 90-day supply. This restriction helps law enforcement agents identify potential dealers. If a person is caught with a large amount of prescription drugs, it is difficult for them to claim all of the pills are for them. It is far more likely that they are intending to sell at least some of the drugs.

There are other restrictions. Refills are not allowed at all, although in some states, doctors are allowed to issue multiple sequential prescriptions. This means that if a doctor decides to prescribe an opioid painkiller for a legitimate reason and knows the patient will need more than one bottle, the doctor can write up to three prescriptions at once, each for a 30-day supply. On each prescription, the doctor must write the earliest date the prescription can be filled, and it is illegal for a pharmacy to fill the prescription before that date. This way of prescribing drugs is more secure than issuing refills because there is no set date for getting a refill. People who are addicted to drugs often take more than they are supposed to at one time, so they run out more quickly and try to get refills more often.

In 2014, in an attempt to make it more difficult for people to abuse hydrocodone, the drug was moved from Schedule III to Schedule II. This included drugs that contain hydrocodone, such as Vicodin. Many doctors and patients with long-term pain were upset by this because it made it much harder for patients to get hydrocodone for legitimate uses. The DEA allowed people with hydrocodone refills to keep refilling their prescriptions after the change happened, but in some places, this conflicted with state laws, so people had to go back to their doctors for new prescriptions. They were also required to check in every 90 days to make sure they were not abusing their medication, and they could no longer call in prescriptions over the phone.

As it has been only a few years since these changes were made, it is uncertain whether they have had a strong impact on the number of people abusing hydrocodone. Other opioids that have been classified as Schedule II for years are still being abused, so it is likely that people who are addicted will find ways to get them. However, the changes did have an immediate negative effect on people who legitimately need pain medication. Dr. Lynn Webster spoke of a former patient feeling the effects of hydrocodone's reclassification:

She lives two hours away from the doctor who currently helps manage her pain. For her, it's a 4-hour round trip every 90 days to access the medication that has helped revive a semblance [of] normalcy since her pain first surfaced when she was just 20 years old. What's worse, she told me that now, more than ever, she has been made to feel like a criminal for seeking

Although there is potential for abuse of strong painkillers, there is still a legitimate need for powerful drugs in long-term pain management.

access to medicine that has been rightfully prescribed to her by her own doctor.[31]

For adults who have jobs, especially jobs without paid personal days, it can be very difficult to get time off work for a visit to the doctor. If they do not have personal days, they are losing money for each hour they spend away from work. Most people also have to pay each time they see a doctor, even if they have insurance.

After the first 100 days of hydrocodone's change from Schedule III to Schedule II, the National Fibromyalgia & Chronic Pain Association (NFMCPA) surveyed chronic pain patients to see how they had been affected. Jan Chambers, president and founder of the NFMCPA, summed up the study's findings:

> *Inadequate attention seems to have been paid to how patients would cope with higher expenditures, difficulty in obtaining an appointment to see their physician every 30 days, feeling like they are being treated as criminals when seeking pain-relieving drugs, and inadequate pain relief or withdrawal symptoms when the 30-day prescription runs out over a weekend or holiday or from a shortage at their designated pharmacy. Survey results also point to discrimination against, and stigmatization of, people suffering with chronic pain.*[32]

No Easy Solution

The recent media attention on the prescription drug crisis, especially in regard to opioids, has been helpful in bringing to light the risks of prescription drug use and abuse, but it has had the unfortunate side effect of creating a stigma around the use of prescription drugs. In other words, some people now view anyone who is taking a potentially addictive prescription drug as being already addicted, even though for many people, these drugs are necessary.

Some people feel that the best solution to the prescription drug crisis is to stop prescribing these drugs completely. Unfortunately, this is not a realistic solution. Opioid painkillers, in particular, are necessary for some people with extremely severe pain. A person with chronic pain has difficulty doing everyday tasks, and if severe pain is left untreated for long enough, it can damage the body and the brain. Experts fear that laws restricting the prescription of painkillers may end up only hurting the people who need them, not the people who are misusing them. According to *Scientific American,*

> *90 percent of all addictions—no matter what the drug—start in the adolescent and young adult years. Typically, young people who misuse prescription opioids are heavy users of alcohol and other drugs. This type of drug use, not medical treatment with opioids, is by far the greatest risk factor for opioid addiction, according to a study by Richard Miech of the University of Michigan and his colleagues.*[33]

The highest risk factors for abuse of prescription drugs are childhood trauma, mental illness, unemployment, and poverty. People who deal with one or more of these issues often turn to drugs to help them deal with their situation, especially if they do not have access to therapy.

One major contributing factor in the prescription drug epidemic, especially in regard to opioids, is problems within the health insurance industry. There are many complex factors that determine insurance prices and coverage, but most people agree that insurance prices are generally higher than the average American can afford, especially if an employer is not paying part of the premium (monthly cost). They are higher than in any other developed country in the world, and many insurance plans have limits as to what is covered. The lower the monthly premium, the fewer things are covered and the higher the out-of-pocket cost for things that are covered, so someone who chooses a plan with a lower premium may not be paying less in the long term.

Many insurance plans cover prescription medications but do not cover therapy to treat mental illness or stress. Even when they do, many therapists do not accept insurance because they find the insurance system difficult and

Massage may help soothe mild-to-moderate muscle pain, but many insurance plans do not cover it.

confusing to manage. Many types of insurance do not cover alternative remedies that might work well for lower levels of pain, such as acupuncture, herbal supplements, chiropractors, or massages. For this reason, doctors may prescribe painkillers because they are easier for people to afford than alternative pain management treatments.

Medical Marijuana: A Safer Alternative?

One proposed solution to part of the prescription drug crisis is for people to turn to medical marijuana. It is being used legally in many states for conditions that opioids and benzodiazepines are currently prescribed to treat, including anxiety, depression, chronic pain, and sleep disorders. Marijuana is not as addictive as opioids or benzodiazepines, and there is evidence to show that it is not often a gateway drug to harder substances, such as heroin or cocaine. Additionally, there have not been any recorded cases of overdose by marijuana.

Marijuana is legal in some states, but the federal government classifies it as a Schedule I substance, and federal rules always take precedence over state rules. Because marijuana is still outlawed by the federal government, it has been very difficult for researchers to study its medical effects. For this reason, the FDA is a long way away from approving it for any kind of medication because the organization only approves medication after clinical trials—scientific studies involving a lot of people taking the drug—have occurred. Clinical trials allow researchers to study how the drug affects men and women, decide whether it is safe for children, and note any side effects that may occur.

Although marijuana has a lower risk of addiction and overdose, it does come with its own health risks that should not be ignored. Young adults, in particular, should not use marijuana because heavy use can cause permanent memory damage to developing brains. The younger a person starts smoking marijuana, the more likely he or she is to develop a dependence on it. Additionally, the active ingredients tetrahydrocannabinol (THC) and cannabidiol (CBD) are not the only chemicals in marijuana; there are more than 500 kinds of chemicals, and it is difficult to predict the ways they will affect each individual. Since the plants grow naturally, it is also difficult to tell how much of each chemical is in each plant. According to NIDA for Teens:

This causes serious problems trying to use the whole marijuana leaf, or crude extracts like hash oil, as medicine:

1. *It's hard to deliver precise, accurate doses of the right chemicals;*

2. *It can harm the lungs if users smoke it; and*

3. *It causes additional effects—like the "high"—that may interfere with the quality of life of patients taking the drug for serious medical conditions.*[34]

Some of these risks can be avoided by changing the method by which marijuana is ingested. For example, taking THC or CBD in pill or oil form does not damage the lungs because no smoke is being inhaled into them. Also, CBD oil may relieve some health issues without causing a high that interferes with a patient's daily life. More research is necessary to determine whether marijuana is as effective at treating health issues as prescription opioids or benzodiazepines.

Another problem with medical marijuana is that health insurance currently does not cover it, which can make it difficult for some people to afford it. A gram of marijuana, which can last up to a week depending on how often the patient is smoking it, typically costs about $10 at a licensed dispensary. A bottle of CBD oil, which can last anywhere from 4 to 14 days depending on the frequency of use, typically costs about $15. The cost of legally obtained prescription drugs depends on many factors, so it is difficult to say whether legally obtained marijuana is cheaper. Someone's insurance may cover generic prescription pills but not name brands; if there is no generic version available, the person will have to pay the entire cost of their medication out of pocket.

Alternatively, someone's insurance may cover the drug, but require the patient to pay a copay. This means that the insurance covers almost all of the price of a bottle of pills, but the patient has to pay a certain amount when he or she picks up the pills. This copay varies from insurance to insurance; one plan may

THE TRAGEDY OF OVERDOSE

Some prescription drugs, especially opioids, are incredibly dangerous because of how easily they can kill the user. If a person takes more pills than he or she is supposed to, or takes them with alcohol or other drugs, the risk of death increases. Opioids and CNS depressants can slow or stop a user's breathing, so there is a risk that a person may simply fall asleep and stop breathing. The drug naloxone can reverse an overdose by attaching to opioid receptors in the brain to block the opioids from attaching. However, naloxone needs to be given as soon as an overdose starts in order to save someone's life.

Superstar entertainer Prince died in April 2016 as a result of taking legally prescribed fentanyl to treat long-term pain. Experts found that fentanyl was the only drug in Prince's body after his death, suggesting he did not mix it with other drugs. Before he died, there were reports that his staff had contacted addiction specialists. Prince's death called attention to the dangers of prescription painkillers and the fact that more Americans than ever before are taking them.

charge a $5 copay for a bottle of pills, while another may charge $20. Some insurance plans may require no copay at all but have a higher monthly premium. A bottle of opioid painkillers or benzodiazepines typically gives the patient a month's supply if he or she is using the medication as directed.

World-famous entertainer Prince died due to an overdose of prescription drugs. This underscored the dangerous potential of powerful pain medications.

Education Is Key

A major part of reducing the number of people addicted to prescription drugs is educating doctors and the general public. Many who abuse prescription drugs believe that anything a doctor prescribes is safe, and many doctors have been given confusing information by drug companies and misleading research. There is no easy or quick way to fix the prescription drug addiction epidemic, but getting people to understand that prescription drugs are dangerous is a good start.

The Substance Abuse and Mental Health Services Administration (SAMHSA) offers a course doctors can take that "provides specific knowledge and skills associated with safely prescribing opioids for chronic pain, and clinical strategies for managing challenging patient situations."[35] Additionally, the CDC issued guidelines "suggesting doctors use non-opioid therapies when possible and, if and when one is needed, to start patients with a lower dose and a shorter supply—a technique that they call 'start low and go slow.'"[36] Other guidelines for doctors include:

- *Be explicit and realistic about expected benefits of opioids, explaining that while opioids can reduce pain during short-term use, there is no good evidence that opioids improve pain or function with long-term use, and that complete relief of pain is unlikely.*

- *Emphasize improvement in function as a primary goal and that function can improve even when pain is still present.*

- *Advise patients about serious adverse effects of opioids, including potentially fatal respiratory depression and development of a potentially serious lifelong opioid use disorder that can cause distress and inability to fulfill major role obligations.*[37]

Similarly, experts advise doctors to be realistic with their patients about the limitations of stimulants and sedatives,

EVALUATING DRUG ADS

It is important for people to know that commercials are designed to sell a product. It is illegal for companies to outright lie about their products, but they may use misleading tactics to sway a person. Some things to watch for in drug commercials include:

- *Ads that target a certain gender.* Are more women or more men featured in the commercial? How much speaking time do men get versus women?

- *Use of visuals to distract from side effects.* When the speaker lists the side effects, does the commercial show a cartoon? This may be intended to create the idea in the viewer's mind that the side effects are not real or serious.

- *Information overload.* When the side effects are listed, does the narrator speak more quickly and use a lot of long words to overwhelm viewers so they stop paying attention?

Being on the lookout for these and other tricks can help consumers stay informed.

emphasizing that they are not magic cures; they simply help patients manage the effects of certain conditions. In recent years, journalists have reported more on the way drug companies market their pills—for instance, instructing drug reps to downplay the seriousness of some side effects when they talk to doctors. Knowing about these tactics can help doctors, patients, and parents be more informed when choosing medication.

With training, doctors can help educate their patients. Drug ads can be found on TV, radio, billboards, online, and in magazines. These are called direct-to-consumer (DTC) ads because previously, drug companies could only market their products to doctors, who would then decide if the drug was right for the patient. Today, many commercials end by urging patients to ask their doctor about a particular drug.

Some people believe this is a good thing because it gives patients more options, but in 2013, ABC News reported that every year, the FDA sends about 100 letters to companies that run ads that "stretch the truth with overstated claims of effectiveness and understated descriptions of side effects ... Some companies are repeat offenders."[38] Because these ads are so often misleading, the United States and New Zealand are the only two countries in the world where DTC advertising is legal for prescription medication. People who see drug ads need to remember that they are made by a company trying to sell a product, so it is always in the company's best interest to make the drug sound as appealing as possible.

Better access to therapy and treatment for mental illness is also crucial. Prescription drugs are cheaper and easier to get than therapy, so many people who could benefit from seeing a psychologist either do not have that option or see a cost benefit to self-medicating. However, limiting access to these drugs would harm the people who need them more than the ones who abuse them because people who have an addiction are often willing to do illegal things to get the drug they are addicted to.

Some people may be more willing to take a drug, either legally or illegally, than go to therapy because there is a stigma surrounding mental illness and those who seek help. Reducing that stigma requires people to change the way they view mental illness in themselves and others, which is something that will not happen overnight.

Looking Toward the Future

Solving the prescription drug epidemic will not be easy. There is no quick fix for this problem. Eliminating prescription drugs is not the answer, as they still help many people with legitimate medical problems. Opioid painkillers are essential in helping people manage severe short-term pain. Benzodiazepines help people control severe anxiety and panic attacks that interfere with their daily life. Stimulants can be useful in controlling ADHD and narcolepsy.

However, all great powers can be abused, and drugs are no different. In the drive to make greater profits, the drug industry has been too quick to put drugs on the market and too eager to have doctors prescribe them for more problems than they should. Doctors, too, have not educated themselves adequately about the dangers of addiction that these drugs possess. However, most of all, the public needs to understand that drugs, even when they come from a doctor, can both cure and kill, help and hurt. No drug is completely safe, and it is just as easy to become addicted to a drug from a pharmacy as it is to a drug from a dealer. Educating the medical community and the general public about the dangers of prescription drugs, as well as decreasing the stigma around addiction, are key to fighting the prescription drug epidemic that the United States is facing.

Notes

Chapter One: The History of Modern Medicine

1. Biljana Bauer Petrovska, "Historical Review of Medicinal Plants' Usage," National Center for Biotechnology Information, *Pharmacognosy Reviews*, vol. 6, issue 11, Jan-June 2012. www.ncbi.nlm.nih.gov/pmc/articles/PMC3358962/.
2. "Drug Scheduling," Drug Enforcement Administration. www.dea.gov/druginfo/ds.shtml.

Chapter Two: The Rise of Prescription Drug Abuse

3. "How Do Opioids Affect the Brain and Body?" National Institute on Drug Abuse, August 2016. www.drugabuse.gov/publications/research-reports/prescription-drugs/opioids/how-do-opioids-affect-brain-body.
4. "Substance Use—Prescription Drugs," Mount Sinai Health System. www.mountsinai.org/health-library/special-topic/substance-use-prescription-drugs.
5. "Substance Use—Prescription Drugs," Mount Sinai Health System.
6. Kelley McMillan, "The Truth About Prescription Pills: One Writer's Story of Anxiety and Addiction," *Vogue*, April 25, 2014. www.vogue.com/865132/prescription-pill-addiction-drug-abuse/.
7. Kate Ashford, "Should You Medicate Your Child Who Has ADHD?" Parents, 2014. www.parents.com/health/add-adhd/should-you-medicate-your-child-who-has-adhd/.
8. Steven Dowshen, MD, "Prescription Drug Abuse," TeensHealth, April 2014. teenshealth.org/en/teens/prescription-drug-abuse.html?WT.ac=ctg.
9. Quoted in "Opioids: Last Week Tonight with John Oliver (HBO)," YouTube video, 19:22, posted by LastWeekTonight, October 23, 2016. www.youtube.com/watch?v=5pdPrQFjo2o.
10. Rachel Ehrenberg, "Published Clinical Trials Shown to Be Misleading," *Science News*, January 29, 2013. www.sciencenews.org/article/published-clinical-trials-shown-be-misleading.

Chapter Three: The Consequences of Addiction

11. McMillan, "The Truth About Prescription Pills: One Writer's Story of Anxiety and Addiction."
12. "Prescription Drugs," NIDA for Teens, December 7, 2016. teens.drugabuse.gov/drug-facts/prescription-drugs.
13. Will Nicoll, "Why Are Women Still Considered More Insane than Men?" *Telegraph*, May 23, 2013. www.telegraph.co.uk/women/womens-life/10048973/Valium-turns-50-Why-are-women-still-considered-more-insane-than-men.html.
14. Steven Nelson, "Buying Drugs Online Remains Easy, 2 Years After FBI Killed Silk Road," *U.S. News & World Report*, October 2, 2015. www.usnews.com/news/articles/2015/10/02/buying-drugs-online-remains-easy-2-years-after-fbi-killed-silk-road.
15. Noel Brennan, "Local Students Bought Drugs from Secret Facebook Group," 9 News, May 4, 2016. www.9news.com/news/local/fly-society-420-facebook-group-drug-sales-/171794439.
16. Melissa Stetten, "Adderall Is the Best and Worst Thing Ever," XO Jane, March 31, 2014. www.xojane.com/issues/adderall-is-the-best-and-worst-thing-ever.
17. Sydney Lupkin, "5 Reasons Prescription Drug Prices Are So High in the U.S.," *TIME*, August 23, 2016. time.com/money/4462919/prescription-drug-prices-too-high/.
18. Lupkin, "5 Reasons Prescription Drug Prices Are So High in the U.S."

Chapter Four: Recovery from Addiction

19. Christine Case-Lo, "Opiate Withdrawal," Healthline, October 20, 2015. www.healthline.com/health/opiate-withdrawal.
20. Case-Lo, "Opiate Withdrawal."
21. Edwin A. Saltisz, MD., "Commentary: Countering the Myths About Methadone," Partnership for Drug-Free Kids, August 6, 2013. www.drugfree.org/news-service/commentary-countering-the-myths-about-methadone/.
22. Salitsz, "Commentary: Countering Myths About Methadone."

23. "The Amphetamine Withdrawal Syndrome," Australian Government Department of Health, April 2004. www.health. gov.au/internet/publications/publishing.nsf/Content/drug-treat-pubs-modpsy-toc~drugtreat-pubs-modpsy-3~drugtreat-pubs-modpsy-3-7~drugtreat-pubs-modpsy-3-7-aws.

24. "The Amphetamine Withdrawal Syndrome," Australian Government Department of Health.

25. "Cognitive-Behavioral Therapy (Alcohol, Marijuana, Cocaine, Methamphetamine, Nicotine)," National Institute on Drug Abuse, December 2012. www.drugabuse.gov/publications/ principles-drug-addiction-treatment-research-based-guide-third-edition/evidence-based-approaches-to-drug-addic-tion-treatment/behavioral.

Chapter Five: The Fight Against Prescription Drug Abuse

26. Carly Putnam, "Opportunity Missed: The Prescription Monitoring Program in Oklahoma," Oklahoma Policy Institute, July 03, 2014. okpolicy.org/opportunity-missed-prescription-monitoring-program-oklahoma/.

27. Shelly Reese, "Drug Abuse Among Doctors: Easy, Tempting, and Not Uncommon," Medscape, January 29, 2014. www.medscape.com/viewarticle/819223.

28. Quoted in Khary K. Rigg, Steven P. Kurtz, and Hilary L. Surratt, "Patterns of Prescription Medication Diversion Among Drug Dealers," National Center for Biotechnology Informa-tion, *Drugs: Education, Prevention and Policy*, vol. 19, no. 2, 2012. www.ncbi.nlm.nih.gov/pmc/articles/PMC3365597/.

29. Liz Welch, "Adderall: The 'Get Ahead' Drug," *Self*, March 11, 2013. www.self.com/story/adderall-the-get-ahead-drug.

30. "Drug Scheduling," Drug Enforcement Administration.

31. Lynn Webster, MD, "DEA Inflicts Harm on Chronic Pain Patients," Lynn Webster, MD. www.lynnwebstermd.com/dea-inflicts-harm-on-chronic-pain-patients/.

32. "Hydrocodone Rescheduling Survey Preliminary Results," National Fibromyalgia and Chronic Pain Association, 2014. www.fmcpaware.org/hydrocodone-rescheduling-survey-preliminary-results.html.

33. Maia Szalavitz, "Opioid Addiction Is a Huge Problem, but Pain Prescriptions Are Not the Cause," *Scientific American* Blog Network, May 10, 2016. blogs.scientificamerican.com/mind-guest-blog/opioid-addiction-is-a-huge-problem-but-pain-prescriptions-are-not-the-cause/.

34. The NIDA Blog Team, "What's Wrong With 'Medical Marijuana'?" NIDA for Teens, September 8, 2014. teens.drugabuse.gov/blog/post/what-s-wrong-medical-marijuana.

35. "SAMHSA's Efforts to Fight Prescription Drug Misuse and Abuse," Substance Abuse and Mental Health Services Administration, March 21, 2016. www.samhsa.gov/prescription-drug-misuse-abuse/samhsas-efforts.

36. "Opioids: Last Week Tonight with John Oliver (HBO)," YouTube video, posted by LastWeekTonight.

37. Deborah Dowell, MD, Tamara M. Haegerich, PhD, and Roger Chou, MD, "CDC Guideline for Prescribing Opioids for Chronic Pain—United States, 2016," Centers for Disease Control and Prevention, March 18, 2016. www.cdc.gov/mmwr/volumes/65/rr/rr6501e1.htm.

38. Jackie Judd, "FDA Calls Prescription Drug Ads Misleading," ABC News. abcnews.go.com/WNT/story?id=131335&page=1.

Addiction Resource Guide
P.O. Box 8612
Tarrytown, NY 10591
(914) 725-5151
info@addictionresourceguide.com
www.addictionresourceguide.com
Some people who are addicted to prescription drugs may benefit from inpatient treatment. This means the patient checks into a
rehabilitation facility for a certain number of days and dedicates all
their time to recovering. The Addiction Resource Guide lists services
and resources to help people who want to recover from an addiction,
as well as a list of contact information for rehab facilities around the
United States.

American Herbal Products Association
8630 Fenton Street
Suite 918
Silver Spring, MD 20910
(301) 588-1171
www.ahpa.org
The American Herbal Products Association is a trade organization
that represents the manufacturers of dietary supplements and acts as
an advocate for the industry during congressional hearings and
similar forums. Visitors to the organization's website can find
press releases and answers to frequently asked questions about
herbal supplements.

Narcotics Anonymous
P.O. Box 9999
Van Nuys, CA 91409
(818) 773-9999
www.na.org
Narcotics Anonymous is a nonprofit organization that helps people
recover from addiction to narcotics. Members support each other in
their recovery by sharing their experiences in group meetings. A list
of meeting locations can be found on the website.

ReachOut USA
109 Stevenson Street
3rd Floor
San Francisco, CA 94105
website@rousa.org
www.reachout.com
This nonprofit organization aims to help young adults through tough times by connecting them with peer support and giving them information on mental health issues. Through the online forum, teens can meet and talk with other teens who are dealing with similar issues, including depression, anxiety, self-harm, drug abuse, and relationship problems.

U.S. Drug Enforcement Administration
DEA Diversion Control Division
Attn: Liaison and Policy Section
8701 Morissette Drive
Springfield, VA 22152
(877) 792-2873
www.dea.gov
The DEA provides information about prescription drugs, including the penalties for dealing them and where and how old prescriptions can be properly disposed of. On the website, people can report online pharmacies that seem illegal as well as suspicious activities by doctors and pharmacists.

Books

Engdahl, Sylvia. *Prescription Drugs.* Farmington Hills, MI: Greenhaven Press, 2014.
Do people take too many prescription drugs today? Why are prescription drug prices so high? What are the main causes of prescription drug abuse, and what can be done to solve the epidemic the United States is currently facing? Engdahl discusses the debates surrounding these and other questions.

Field, Jon Eben. *Depression and Other Mood Disorders.* New York, NY: Crabtree Publishing Company, 2014.
People who suffer from anxiety, depression, and other mood disorders may begin to abuse painkillers and benzodiazepines to help themselves feel better. This increases their risk of developing a psychological dependency on the drug—feeling like they must have it in order to feel better. Learning the symptoms of mood disorders and how to properly treat them can decrease the risk of dangerous self-medicating.

Goldsmith, Connie. *Dietary Supplements: Harmless, Helpful, or Hurtful?* Minneapolis, MN: Twenty-First Century Books, 2016.
Some people believe that dietary supplements are better because they are natural, but is this actually true? Connie Goldsmith is a registered nurse who explores the world of dietary supplements and the ways people use them—hoping for weight loss, enhanced performance in sports, ways to boost energy, and more. Doctors and dieticians give their opinions on supplements, what to watch out for, and whether or not they actually work.

Waters, Rosa. *ADHD Medication Abuse: Adderall, Ritalin, and Other Addictive Stimulants.* Broomall, PA: Mason Crest, 2015. People who abuse Adderall and other stimulants are likely to get those pills from friends who have ADHD. Many people believe that because a drug has been prescribed to one person, it is safe for everyone to take. Waters dispels that myth and discusses the issues that arise when people take stimulants they have not been prescribed.

Waters, Rosa. *Prescription Painkillers: Oxycontin, Percocet, Vicodin, and Other Addictive Analgesics.* Broomall, PA: Mason Crest, 2015. Painkillers can have dangerous physical side effects and are highly addictive. This book discusses some of the most common painkillers and their unintended as well as intended effects.

Websites

Above the Influence
abovetheinfluence.com
Young adults can find facts about prescription and street drugs from medical professionals, read blog posts containing advice from other young adults, and add their own opinions about drug abuse to the website.

Live Science
www.livescience.com
Searches for "prescription drugs" or the specific name of some drugs provide many informed articles on these issues. Some topics include facts about different types of prescription drugs and the latest news concerning the prescription drug epidemic.

The National Suicide Prevention Lifeline
suicidepreventionlifeline.org
(800) 273-8255 (1-800-273-TALK)
Prescription drug abuse is often a way for someone to deal with emotional pain. The National Suicide Prevention Lifeline provides free, confidential crisis support for anyone who is considering suicide for any reason. A live chat is also available through the website.

NIDA for Teens
www.teens.drugabuse.gov
This website, a project of the National Institute on Drug Abuse, is designed specifically for middle and high schoolers who have questions about drug use and abuse, as well as more in-depth looks at the neuroscience of drug use.

7 Cups of Tea
www.7cups.com
Using the app or the website, people can reach out to an anonymous listener to discuss problems both big and small. The listeners do not judge, solve problems, or give advice; they affirm emotions and give users a safe place to vent their feelings. There are also peer chat rooms and resources that help people find a licensed therapist, either online or in their area.

G

gamma-aminobutyric acid (GABA), 28

H

Halcion, 28
Harrison Narcotics Tax Act, 20
health insurance, 48, 55, 57, 69, 72, 79–85
herbal supplements, 15, 18, 82
heroin, 6–7, 20–21, 24, 41, 60, 67, 82
hydrocodone, 13, 24, 77, 79

I

insomnia, 8–9, 27, 31, 66
insurance fraud, 57, 69, 72

J

Jobs, Steve, 16
Journal of Addiction Medicine, 74

K

ketamine, 18
kidney failure, 16
Klonopin, 42–43

L

laudanum, 20
leeches, use of in early medicine, 11
Lortab, 13
LSD, 8, 52

M

marijuana, 8, 41, 43, 52, 82–83
McMillan, Kelley, 42–43
MDMA, 8, 14, 52
medicine, turning point in, 13
mental health treatment, women versus men, 45–46
meperidine, 24
Merck, 14

methadone, 64–65, 74
methamphetamine, 31, 41, 52–53, 66
methylphenidate, 31
Monitoring the Future surey, 7
morphine, 17, 20, 24, 36, 48
Mrs. Winslow's Soothing Syrup, 17

N

naloxone, 84
narcotic, 20, 68
Narcotics Anonymous, 68
National Fibromyalgia & Chronic Pain Association (NFMCPA), 79
National Institute on Drug Abuse (NIDA)
on abuse of cough syrup, 18
Monitoring the Future survey and, 7
on opioid receptors, 26
NIDA for Teens
on commonly abused substances, 43
on medical marijuana, 83
natural versus synthetic argument, 15–16
neurotransmitter, 28, 33, 66
New York State, 72
norepinephrine, 33

O

Oklahoma Policy Institute, 71
opium, 13, 17, 20, 25
optimism bias, 46
overdose, 8, 27–28, 34, 58, 82, 84–85
over-the-counter (OTC), 18
over-the-counter drug abuse, 18
oxycodone, 24, 55–56, 60
OxyContin, 22, 24, 39, 56, 60, 72

P

paranoia, 35
Partnership for Drug-Free Kids, 65

patent medicines, 17–18
performance-enhancing drugs, 10, 35
Perry, Matthew, 21
Pfizer, 39
phencyclidine (PCP), 18
poppy, 13, 20
prescribing off-label, 39
prescription drugs
  babies born addicted to, 67
  categories of, 20, 27
  CDC report on Americans' use of, 21
  cost of, 55–57, 60, 80, 83–85
  Drugs: Education, Prevention and Policy journal study on, 74
  effects on the brain, 10, 27–28, 33–34
  effects on society, 57–58
  false information on, 37, 39–40
  Harvard Medical School study on, 56–57
  health care definitions of problems relating to, 54
  insurance fraud, 57, 69, 72
  the Internet and, 50–52
  Journal of Addiction Medicine study on, 74
  medical marijuana as alternative to, 82–83
  mixing of, 41
  myths about, 26, 30, 35
  rate of use among 12th graders, 7, 44
  rate of use compared to illegal drugs, 8
  reasons for use, 8
  risk factors for addiction, 43, 45, 80
  risk of heroin abuse due to, 41, 60
  side effects, 16, 26, 28, 40, 87–88
  signs of addiction to, 29
  stigma of, 79
  TIME magazine on, 56
  versus addiction to illegal drugs, 6–7, 42, 67

Washington Post on heroin and, 60
Prescription Monitoring Program (PMP), 71
Prince, 84–85
Prozac, 16
Purdue, 39, 56, 72

R
recovery, 10, 58, 61–69
relapse, 27, 62–63, 66, 68
Ritalin, 9, 31, 33–34, 48, 66, 76
Robitussin, 18
robotripping, 18

S
schedules for drugs, 20, 72, 76–77, 79, 82
Science News, 39
Scientific American, 80
sedatives, 8–9, 45, 48, 86
seizures, 29, 35, 67
serotonin, 66
Silk Road, 52
Soska, Kyle, 52
steroids, 35
Stetten, Melissa, 52–53
stimulants, 9, 20, 23, 30–33, 35, 41, 43, 45, 48, 52, 66–67, 76, 86, 89
St. John's wort, 15–16
suboxone, 64
Substance Abuse and Mental Health Services Administration (SAMHSA), 86

T
TeensHealth, 34
Thomas, David, 37
TIME magazine, 56
tolerance, 24, 27, 31, 47
tranquilizers, 7–8, 20, 23, 27, 45
treatment
  decision to get, 58, 61
  detoxification during, 64

Simon Pierce grew up in Jamestown, New York. He later moved to New York City and completed his education at NYU. He now lives in Brooklyn with his partner and their son. He has written for various health and wellness publications over the past seven years. He and his family enjoy people-watching in the park as well as reading the names on cemetery headstones and inventing stories about them.